The Daily T[elegraph]

Buying a Pro[perty in]
Italy

Other related titles published by How To Books

Going to Live in Italy
Your practical guide to the nitty gritty of settling in

Getting a Job Abroad
The International Jobseekers' Directory

Retire Abroad
Your complete guide to a new way of life in the sun

Going to Live in Greece
Your practical guide to life and work in Greece

Please send for a free copy of the latest catalogue to:
How To Books
3 Newtec Place, Magdalen Road,
Oxford OX4 1RE, United Kingdom
email: info@howtobooks.co.uk
www.howtobooks.co.uk

The Daily Telegraph
Buying a Property in
Italy

*An insider guide to finding
a home in the sun*

AMANDA HINTON

howtobooks

Published in 2003 by
How To Books Ltd, 3 Newtec Place,
Magdalen Road, Oxford OX4 1RE,
United Kingdom.
Tel: (01865) 793806. Fax: (01865) 248780.
email: info@howtobooks.co.uk
www.howtobooks.co.uk

First edition 2003

British Library Cataloguing in Publication Data
A catalogue record for this book is available from
the British Library.

Cover design by Baseline Arts Ltd, Oxford
Casa Santoni, featured on the front cover, is just
one of the many beautiful properties sold through
www.holidayhome.co.uk
Line drawings by Nicki Averill

Produced for How To Books by Deer Park Productions
Typeset by Anneset, Weston-super-Mare, North Somerset
Printed and bound by Cromwell Press, Trowbridge, Wiltshire

NOTE: The material contained in this book is set out in good
faith for general guidance and no liability can be accepted
for loss or expense incurred as a result of relying in particular
circumstances on statements made in the book. The laws and
regulations are complex and liable to change, and readers should
check the current position with the relevant authorities before
making personal arrangements.

Contents

Note from the Author

Buying a property in Italy is neither more nor less difficult than in the UK, but the system is different, and therefore it is best to be well informed before making any decisions or commitments. You will find that the better informed you are, the easier it will be to jump the bureaucratic hurdles that will inevitably present themselves.

At the same time as adjusting to a new system you will also be changing your lifestyle, as Italian homes are tailored to local lifestyles and to the Italian climate. If you are moving into a rural house you will probably find you live on the first floor, which avoids the problem of damp. The ground floor is generally used as garage space and storage. Bathrooms will all have bidets – the Italians regard the British bidet-less bathroom with horror – and the windows will be shuttered, allowing greater control over light and temperature inside the house, especially in the summer, when it becomes very hot. Floors are generally tiled, and so you will have to give up the ubiquitous fitted carpets of British homes, and adapt to the hard beauty of terracotta, stone, ceramic or parquet floors. You may also have to get used to running all your household appliances on a meagre allowance of three kilowatts.

This book prepares you for setting up home in Italy, guiding you through the bureaucratic labyrinth and helping you cope with everyday life, especially those aspects connected with your Italian property. There is information on all facets of buying, from how to find properties to legal procedures. Those intending to renovate property will find a wealth of practical information relevant to the DIY enthusiast and to getting involved in a lengthy architect's project.

I hope you will find this book a useful reference guide, both before you leave and after you arrive in Italy. *Auguri!*

Amanda Hinton

1

Introducing Italy

ITALIAN DREAM

Nowhere in the world is the art of everyday living celebrated in more style than it is in Italy. Lifestyle is the present-day art form of the Italians, echoing their glorious past and applauding modernism. To dream of owning a property there, is to yearn nostalgically for the past whilst appreciating the Latin passion for all things new. Every town has an ancient sunlit piazza waiting to vibrate to the roar of a shiny new red Ferrari. Lamborghini tractors furrow landscapes, timeless as the background of a Renaissance painting. Italian daily life is filled to the brim with the rich mix of history and high tech. In Italy, *la vita è dolce* – life is sweet.

Living Italian style

Who but the Italians could inhabit this glorious country? As volatile and splendid as the land they inhabit, the Italians move with consummate ease through modern-day life. Builders sing Verdi arias as they pour cement, drivers cause traffic jams outside the *chiesa* as they wait to have their car blessed on the patron saint's day of travellers. There is a glorious continuity of chaos throughout the country.

As they live so do they dress, with a flair for fashion that is as genetic as their respect for fine food. At the end of the working day, the Italian world and his wife enjoy *l'ora della passeggiata*, the hour for promenade, passing back and forth, admiring each other in the setting sun. Past masters at cutting a dash, *la bella figura*, is a crucial part of every true Italian's image-conscious life.

Whilst the rest of the world is rushing down the fast lane to junk food, the Italians celebrate at slow food festivals. The ritual of selecting, preparing and cooking food is close to religion. An hour can easily be devoted to arguing over the best recipe for a *carbonara* sauce.

Time is magically divided between endless patience and urgent speed. The Italians have taken the last minute rush into an art form. Life is clicked into place by ingenuity and their faith in *il destino* – plus any number of happy accidents on the way.

Italy, the schoolroom and playground of the world, offers free lessons in everyday living. In the immortal words of Dr Johnson, 'A man who has not been to Italy is always conscious of an inferiority.'

Café society

Where better to sit and watch the world go by than in an Italian café? Even the smallest towns boast the elegance of marble-clad cafés with whistling espresso machines and gleaming ice-cream counters. Italian coffee, now drunk in cafés all over the world, never tastes better than in Italy. The wide selection of ways to drink it, however, have not all been exported. Where but in Italy could they invent a Valentine's day cappuccino with a heart traced into the drift of chocolate on the frothy spume?

Early on a winter's morning you will hear the air ring with demands for a *caffè corretto* – a spoonful of strong black espresso laced with a nip of local brandy – guaranteed to warm up the start to the working day. Hovering around the bar, joking with their friends, too rushed to sit down, the working Italians delicately snatch up a *pasta*, a light flaky pastry, in a paper napkin and their breakfast is completed in moments. When the early morning rush has suddenly gone, the *caffè* will be left to the hard core of regulars reading the newspapers and summoning up energy for a game of chess or some light gossip. The next flood of customers comes at noon, as the aperitif hour strikes. Spumante, cocktails – alcoholic or otherwise – are served. Small saucers of olives and nuts appear and the morning's business is avidly discussed. The *caffè* will soon begin to empty again as the Italians retreat to the real business of lunch. The pattern of the *caffè* repeats itself like clockwork, as the customers integrate their brief moments of refreshment into the long working day... and around serious meals.

Eating out

It is very difficult to eat badly in a restaurant in Italy. Whether stopping whilst travelling in an unknown area, or booking a table in a renowned restaurant, expectations run high and are usually fulfilled, if not exceeded.

The three main styles of eating places are the traditional *ristorante*, *trattoria* or *pizzeria*. The only disappointment you may have, if any, is that of finding the place unexpectedly closed, especially in rural areas. *Pizzerie*, in particular those with *forno di legno*, wood-fired ovens, are usually opened for evening meals only. *Trattorie* and the more formal *ristorante* can both surprise and disappoint with the days and times they elect to close – particularly during the month of August.

Choosing where to eat may be best judged on the basis of the number of cars outside and local people thronging the tables inside. Décor is often low on the list of priorities, although service and cleanliness are highly regarded. If you are lucky enough to have been invited out by Italian friends, you may

3

wish to attempt to split the bill, *alla Romana*, although Italians are notoriously generous and proudly hospitable.

A ten per cent service charge is now generally included in the total bill. Inspection of *il conto* (the bill) will show *coperto* (cover charge per person) and *servizio* (service charge), and any further gratuity is at your discretion and state of euphoria on the completion of the meal.

Sunday lunch is the high-point of the week in Italian restaurants, when large families gather to celebrate the art of eating out. To the outsider, it is more than just a culinary experience. It is an opportunity to watch a lively scene of three and four generations intermingling. Teenagers tenderly escorting their elderly *nonna* whilst dressed from head to toe in black Armani – toddlers dressed to charm as they wolf their way through the *grissini* – sultry young beauties with eyes dark from the memory of Saturday night at the disco – fathers attempting to be strict and, with her eagle eye on them all, *Mamma* – the figurehead of the matriarchal society that is Italy.

Markets

To wander though an Italian market is one of life's simple pleasures. Large or small every Italian market is a spectacle. As the Italian proverb says, *Tre donne e un pollo fanno un mercato* – three women and a chicken make a market.

Il Giorno di mercato (market day) transforms every small town in Italy. A sleepy piazza, which may be little more than a car park for the rest of the week, suddenly becomes the *piazza del mercato* (the market place) and a hive of activity. The market stall-holders roll into town before 8 a.m. and begin to open their vast vans of goods. Space is intelligently allocated, with the coolest areas for fish and meat, surrounded by fresh vegetables and fruit, and every other available square metre being filled with stalls of clothes, shoes, handbags and household goods.

Bargaining is friendly enough but not very fruitful until high noon approaches and the stall-holders are anticipating their well-

4

earned lunch. The air becomes filled with the smell of hot food. The regional specialities, reflecting the seasons, and cooked before your very eyes are surely the best take-away food known to the hungry shopper.

It would be quite possible to spend an entire week in any of the large Italian cities going from one *mercato all'aperto* (outdoor market) to another, and still miss out on something special. Each city has a list of daily markets, which it is wise to study before you set off. Try Rome's Sunday morning *mercato delle pulci* (flea market) at the Porta Portese, the vast fish market in Venice, the colourful market of Padua, stretching down each side of Il Salone, or the fabulous craft market in the Piazza San Lorenzo, Florence, where you will find craft objects in leather, silk, linen, paper and gold.

In the height of the holiday season, which in the top three cities of Florence, Rome and Venice can be nearly all year round, the markets are swamped with tourists accompanied by the inevitable *scippatori* (pickpockets). To go with a good will – and a safe purse – or not at all, is the best solution.

PAST AND PRESENT

The beginnings

The history of Italy, as the country it is known as today, has to begin in 1815 with the fall of Napoleon. After hundreds of years of foreign dominance, Italy finally emerged as a unified kingdom. But Italy would not be the Italy the world loves and enjoys without its glorious ancient past.

Vulnerable to sea attack along its long coastlines and to land attack across its northern mountains, it is not surprising that Italy's history is peppered with foreign invasions. It would be wrong to assume, though, that Italy's geography has always been a disadvantage. The invaders did not always bring havoc and destruction but were often assimilated into Italian society, enriching and diversifying it. Its location at the centre of the

5

Mediterranean also gave the Italian maritime cities a head start in early European trade.

The earliest waves of migrants, dating from the second millennium BC, brought Alpine people from the north, who then integrated with the indigenous Neolithic peoples. At the same time as this, groups of highly cultured people were infiltrating from Greece and Asia Minor, some of whom might have been the ancestors of the Etruscans, the most powerful of Italy's early civilisations. Their culture bears more than a passing resemblance to that of the Lycians in Asia Minor, but whether indigenous or migrant, much of their cultural identity was passed onto the Romans, who succeeded them.

Classical times

The Roman Republic ruled from 509 BC up until 31 BC, after which the Roman Empire, ruled by a series of all-powerful emperors, expanded its dominion over most of the known world. The scale of the Empire's engineering feats grew with its wealth and power. Vestiges remain today, bearing witness to the monumentality of its works. In 380 AD, the Emperor Theodosius converted the state to Christianity, and Rome became the seat of the highest bishop. The real centre of power moved eastwards to Constantinople and Italy's sublime reign of power was nearly at an end.

The dissolution of the Roman Empire around AD 476 gradually led to the break up of Italy into numerous small states. The Byzantine emperors clung to remnants of the Empire for as long as they could, but invasions by the Lombards and Franks, which started around AD 500, wrested Northern Italy from their control.

Great eras

The mediaeval era saw a succession of wars between foreign kings, greedy popes and local dukes alike, so that Northern Italy was by and large a patchwork of petty states.

By the fourteenth century Italy was the most divided and invaded country in Europe although, surprisingly, this turbulent climate not only produced a mass of excellent mediaeval art and architecture but also spawned the Renaissance. This, perhaps the greatest period in Italian history, reached its peak during the sixteenth century. The sack of Rome by Charles V in 1527 signalled, like the tolling of a bell, the symbolic end of the Renaissance.

In the centuries that followed, Northern Italy was continually fought over by the French, Austrian and Spanish, and by the eighteenth century, power was concentrated in the north in the hands of the Hapsburg dynasty in Lombardy, and King Carlo Alberto in Piedmont. Their rule offered security and brought about a period of intellectual enlightenment, which gradually fuelled a movement towards a united Italy.

Towards unification

The rule of the next king of Piedmont, Vittorio Emanuele II, was extended after Garibaldi, who had won control over the southern part of the peninsula, handed it to him in 1861. Vittorio Emanuele II was then proclaimed King of Italy, although complete unification was not achieved until 1870 when Italian troops captured Rome.

The nineteenth century found Italy somewhat behind other countries in Europe in terms of living standards and industrial development and, although improvements were attempted, the instability of the government and breakdowns in law and order meant that little ground was gained.

World wars

During the turbulent period after World War I, the Italian Fascist party, headed by Mussolini, was born. Quickly rising to power, Mussolini ruled Italy from 1922 to 1943, taking it into World

War II on the side of the Germans. Italy was liberated again after allied troops, who had landed at Anzio in 1944, gradually fought their way up through the peninsula. In 1946, a government mainly formed of Christian Democrats took control of the Italian republic, and large companies first established under Mussolini, such as Fiat and Olivetti, put Italy back on the road to economic prosperity. In 1956 it joined the European Economic Community, and from 1959 to 1962 experienced an 'economic miracle', thanks mainly to the large reserves of cheap labour available in southern Italy. Labour conditions and the social changes in the 1960s led to revolutions, strikes and student protests in the 70s. However, in the 80s, Italy seemed to have put many of its problems behind it, and in the 90s, was rated as the fifth leading industrial country in the developed world.

Italy today

Economics
In 1992, Italy had the largest budget deficit in the world, amounting to 11 per cent of its total economic output. However, by raising VAT rates and exercising stringent budget controls, it accomplished the feat of meeting European Union requirements for entry into European Monetary Union in 1997. In the following years, the growth rate in the Italian economy excelled most other European countries. In fact, the statistics are misleading regarding general national wealth due to the continuing huge disparity between the industrial north and the struggling south. In 2001, the growth rate began a serious slowdown due to an increase in public spending, and the looming future budget deficit is likely to be too hefty to meet the European guidelines. The 'hidden economy' also has to be taken into account. The Euro replaced the much-loved lira as the legal currency of Italy on 1 January 2002. It quickly gained in strength against the pound sterling and, although fluctuating daily, now hovers between approximately 1.57 and 1.61 Euros to the pound sterling.

Employment

In July 2001, the National Statistics Bureau announced the Italian unemployment rate to have dropped slowly but surely from 11.4% to a miraculous 9.2%. There has been considerable debate and scepticism about how this figure was reached, and the growth in the economy is said to reflect the introduction of more flexible work contracts – especially in the professional sector and service industries. Competition for work remains high.

Politics

At the head of the state is the President of the Republic, elected for a seven-year term, and in control of the judiciary and the armed forces. The President's power could be compared with that of the British monarch, principally ceremonial but with the final authority to dissolve parliament, pass or veto new laws or dismiss an elected Prime Minister. The Government is seated in the capital city of Rome and parliament comprises two chambers, the *Camera dei Deputati* (Chamber of Deputies) and the *Senato* (Senate). As both chambers hold equal powers, there are frequent and continuing conflicts over parliamentary bills. However, debate is surprisingly less boisterous than in the notoriously rowdy House of Commons in London. Italian women members represented less than 10 per cent in both houses in the 2001 election.

The extremely complicated system of proportional representation, with most of the candidates being unknown to the voter, allows for major political figures or popular celebrities to stand for several constituencies at the same time. It is perfectly legal, and frequently the custom, for a lesser-known candidate to step in at the last moment and take up the votes for a landslide victory.

For a country that normally changes its Prime Minister every nine months, the continuity of the term of office of Silvio Berlusconi, elected in 2001 after the victory of his centre-right bloc coalition, promises a more stable and realistic economy. Berlusconi pledged 'a new era' for Italians, proclaiming 'I am convinced that you all feel the need for a government that governs and of a premier who speaks less and works more and better.'

LIE OF THE LAND

Landscapes

The land mass of Italy is bordered by France, Switzerland, Austria and Slovenia and, including its many islands, occupies an area of 301,278 square kilometres (116,00 square miles). The boot that makes up mainland Italy dips its toe in the Mediterranean, has the Adriatic on its eastern flank, the Tyrrhenian on the west and the Ionian Sea to the south. The coast, including the islands of Sardinia and Sicily, is 7,420 km long. Sicily, the largest of the Italian islands, lies just off the toe of the boot, across the Straits of Messina. The Mediterranean island of Sardinia, the next largest island, has one of the lowest population densities of Italy.

Mountains make up 35.2 per cent of the country. The Alps and Dolomites in the north hang over the series of magnificent lakes and below lies the flat, fertile plain of the River Po. The Apennine Mountains bound the southern edge of the plain. This impressive range runs southwards down the length of the peninsula, like the spine of Italy, ending in the rugged mountainous region of the Abruzzo where brown bears still survive.

Gently folding hills cover just over 40 per cent of the rest of the land. The epitome of the foreigner's romantic vision of Italy, found in the red-earth Tuscan hills dotted with cypress trees, is but a small part of the rich *paesaggio* (landscape).

Where Italians live

For purposes of administration, Italy is divided into 20 regions: Piedmont, Aosta, Lombardy, Trentino-Alto Adige, Veneto, Friuli-Venezia Giulia, Liguria, Emilia Romagna, Tuscany, Umbria, Marche, Lazio, Abruzzo, Molise, Puglia, Campania, Basilicata, Calabria, Sicily and Sardinia. The regions are further subdivided, and comprise 95 provinces with over 8,000 municipalities.

The population of Italy, at approximately 58 million, is slightly higher than that of the UK. With an average of 190 persons per square kilometre they enjoy more space than the British average of 232 persons per square kilometre. With the surprising but undeniable drop in birth rate, the lowest in Europe, there will be even more space in the future, although the shrinkage brings a threat of labour shortages that could threaten the economy. The much debated north–south divide issue continues to worsen and, despite various inducements to develop the south, the industrial north is still dominant.

Climate zones

Italy has many climates and it is advisable to visit the region of your choice at different times of the year. Whereas any foreigner expects ice and snow in the high Alps, it may come as a sharp shock to find a hilltop village in lush green Umbria as cold as Stockholm in the winter.

It has to be said that local inhabitants around the world are notoriously unreliable when reporting their own weather. A wet day in August is always *'non normale'* and the jolly British hope that the sky is definitely brightening does not translate. With the first gust of winter wind, the Italians retreat behind their scarves and scurry around gloomily.

The main industrial areas in the north, spread on the plains of Lombardy, are cold and wet in winter. The northern Italians escape up to the cold but dry Alps for *una settimana bianca* (a week of skiing) or to the milder climate of the Ligurian coast and the pleasures of the Italian Riviera.

The central regions of Tuscany, Umbria and Le Marche have a more temperate climate, which has made them popular with expatriates. Again, it should be noted that the higher areas, certainly anything above 600 metres altitude, might well be snowbound for several winter weeks.

Southern Italy and Sicily enjoy a wonderfully warm winter climate but the height of summer can be scorching hot.

Mother Nature is a reliable guide when house hunting. A close look at the natural vegetation gives a good indication of the climate. If you are seeking the quintessential olive groves, vines and cypresses, then it is best not to buy a house in an area of chestnut forest.

ART AND CULTURE

In the world of art, Italy enjoys an embarrassment of riches. Tuscany alone has more classified historical monuments than any other country in the world.

Architecture

The classical architecture of the Roman Empire has influenced Western architecture for more than two millennia. The Emperor Augustus Caesar declared that he had found Rome built of brick and left it in marble. He could have added that he had bound it together with concrete and so changed the course of architectural history. The Romans discovered this magic mix of natural cement and inert aggregate materials, and the Italians have been pouring it liberally ever since.

One of the most famous buildings in the world is the Pantheon in Rome, commissioned by the Emperor Hadrian, and built in 118–128. The vast dome of 43.2 metres diameter has an oculus (circular opening) of 8.8 metres, which provides the only source of interior light to the rotunda. To take a short walk from the Pantheon, past the massive Colosseum and into the Forum, with its impressive remains of private and public buildings, is a graphic lesson in town planning and the history of architecture. This rich legacy has not been wasted on the Italians. An illustrious list of Italian architects followed in the Roman footsteps.

One, Filippo Brunelleschi, born in Florence in 1377, was a key figure in the progress from the Middle Ages into the Renaissance and the rebirth of the classical form. His introduction of architecture based on the use of linear perspective, the preparation of ground plans, elevations and overall proportional balance of a building has its influences on architecture today. His most impressive engineering feat is seen in the soaring Duomo, built in 1418 over the Gothic cathedral in Florence.

The architecture of the glorious Renaissance era had begun, and who better to take up the work than Michelangelo Buonarroti (1475–1564), the epitome of Renaissance man? Employed by the Popes of Rome, Michelangelo's heart belonged to Florence. His extraordinarily prolific working life endowed Italy with many works of art and architecture. The diversity of his talents as an architect are shown, for example, in the contrast between the elegant Laurentian Library, adjoining San Lorenzo, in Florence, which ignored classical precedents and exuded the forceful energy that is expressed in his painting and sculpture, and his Campidoglio on the Capitoline Hill in Rome, which preserved the tradition of classic Roman monumentality. Built in an oval around the famous bronze equestrian statue of Marcus Aurelius, the latter buildings remain the civic and political heart of the city of Rome.

In the words of the much-travelled Mark Twain, 'Lump the whole thing! Say the Creator made Italy from designs by Michelangelo!' In modern and post-modern Italy, architecture has moved bravely ahead. The engineering ingenuity of Italian architects lives on and is evident in their dramatic use of glass and steel. Anyone who has arrived at the train station in

Florence will have witnessed a fine example of inter-war architecture. There is little or no nostalgic addiction to the neo-classicism found in the housing estates of Britain. With evidence of the real thing all around them, Italians have no need for déjà vu.

Museums

In a country with more than three million exhibits tucked away in museums, the only time that a complaint can ever be heard from the avid 'culture vulture' is when there is a sign '*chiuso*' (closed) on the museum door.

Before setting out, it is wise to make a quick check with the local ENIT tourist office, rather than risk the frustration of being almost in sight of one of the world's treasures. Restoration, or other more obscure reasons, frequently close the museum doors but, generally, Monday is the national closing day.

The Vatican is the superb exception to the rule. Covering more than 40 hectares, it houses one of the richest collections of art treasures in the world. If you arrive at opening time, grab one of the first tickets of the day and run straight to the Sistine Chapel, then you may be just ahead of the hordes of guided tours on your heels. From thereon, the task is to refrain from trying to see everything. In this, the Vatican museum reflects the rest of Italy and its treasure trove.

Galleries

Italian art galleries suffer from the same erratic opening hours as museums, so once again it is advisable to check with the local tourist office. Most Italian churches have enough art treasures hanging on their walls to make them resemble art galleries, but visitors should remember to treat their religious services with respect. When visiting cathedrals with important works of art, take a handful of coins to operate lights and phone guides.

One of the world's greatest collections, rich in Italian and

Flemish art, is housed in the Galleria degli Uffizi, Florence. Here hang the paintings that are reproduced a billion times. Naturally, the most famous paintings bring the longest entry queues, but an improved system of staged ticketing has now been instigated.

The only problem with the art of Italy is that a lifetime is not long enough to view it all.

Opera

Where else could opera have been born than in Italy? An art form that perfectly suits the Italian temperament, with their love of sentiment, melodrama and burlesque... it is in their lifeblood.

The first operatic masterpiece, *Orfeo*, was written by Monteverdi (1567–1643), for the Gonzaga court at Mantua. The fashion spread like wildfire and the pleasure-loving Venetians soon had eleven opera houses running simultaneously. The baton was next taken up by Cavalli (1602–76), and the baroque opera scene soon moved to Naples.

The light melodious trio, Rossini, Bellini and Donizetti, introduced the *bel canto* style, with the naïve plots and heart-rending arias that demanded a prima donna. Verdi (1813–1901), changed the scene again, introducing stronger, more credible plots, ingenious rhythms and sparkling orchestration. His operas – *Rigoletto*, *Aida*, *Il Trovatore*, *La Traviata*, and more – have been, for more than a century, the epitome of grand opera as it is known and loved today.

FOOD AND WINE

What Italians eat

The taste and aroma of *la cucina italiana* has wafted its way into kitchens and restaurants all over the world. Dieticians and health experts expound theories on a balanced regime that every Italian has known about intuitively since birth. There is no doubt that the people of Italy simply know when and how and what to eat. From first thing in the morning to last thing at night they enjoy a disciplined amplitude. The typical meal is composed of several courses. The *antipasto* (starter) is designed to tickle the taste buds – at its simplest it may be a slice or two of salami and *prosciutto crudo* with a few olives and pickled vegetables or, in the summer, a slice of chilled melon or a few ripe figs. A serious restaurant may be famous for a table groaning with a selection of sixty or more *antipasto* delicacies. The experienced eater will either make this the entire meal or choose with moderation. The next course, *il primo*, depending on season and region, may be a *minestra* (vegetable soup), *risotto* or the world-famous *pasta*. The latter comes in an infinite variety of shapes and sizes. Every Italian knows innately which sauce to serve with which shape and whether to dust it with *parmigiano* (parmesan cheese) or whether that is completely the wrong thing to do. Gnocchi, small light potato flour dumplings, accompanied by a rich sauce, are also served as a first course, especially in the winter months. *Polenta*, made from maize, is often the favoured substitute for pasta, particularly in the northern regions. *Il secondo*, (the main course) is served next – either *pesce* (fish) or *carne* (meat) – usually simply cooked and with little accompaniment except a mixed or green salad. Fruit or cheese ends the meal, sweet desserts being reserved for special occasions.

This may seem a daunting amount of food but Italians usually eat each course with moderation and never ever snack between meals. It is true that a mid-morning hunger pang may be assuaged with a slice of thin *pizza* but that could be considered a late breakfast. In fact, *la nuova cucina*, the Italian version of the French nouvelle cuisine, has bitten into the traditional meal, and it is now quite forgivable to skip one or other of the courses.

Drinks

Most of Italy is wine country and Italians revel in their local wine. Happy to enjoy the year's vintage from a local vineyard, even the top restaurateurs respect an honest wine with a provenance known to them personally. Their taste buds are educated and they are unlikely to succumb to the snobbery attached to a famous label. Drinking wine at a young age is an accepted part of the culture. Despite, or maybe because of this, Italians are not a nation of heavy drinkers. To be *ubriaco* (drunk) carries the stigma of disapproval amongst the majority of Italians. Alcohol sales have dropped as sales of mineral water have increased. Statistics also show a significant rise in the sales of beer, as the young Italians become more cosmopolitan.

Any large feast will be followed with an offer of a *digestivo* to settle the stomach before retiring. There is an inspirational selection from Cynar, made from artichokes, to Grappa, made from the residue of stalks, pips and skins of pressed grapes. If politeness forces you to accept a small glass of your host's own grappa and the first sip brings tears to your eyes, it is socially acceptable to tip it into your coffee.

Ice-creams

Italian ice-cream is enjoyed all over the world but there is nowhere better to eat it than in an Italian *gelateria* (ice-cream parlour). Whether you want a simple *cono* (cone) or *coppa* (tub) or a frivolous *gelato con panna* (ice-cream topped with whipped cream), you can be sure that the ice-cream will be of top quality. Italians often go to a *gelateria* after the cinema or theatre, and you may need to know that a *gelato affogato* is an ice-cream drowned in whisky. A *semi-freddo* is any confection from a frozen mousse to an ice-cream cake. *Granita*, a refreshing drink of flavoured ice crystals, is an ideal way to cool down in the heat of summer. A serious *gelateria* will concoct a tempting selection of ice-cream cakes which are an ideal gift to take to any Italian host that has invited you to the delights of dining *da noi*, at their home.

SUMMARY

The varied scenic landscape with its dramatic regional and climatic changes has impacted on the inhabitants and their daily lives. A Milanese is a long distant relation to a Napolitano but all Italians have a highly developed sense of national and local pride. The Italian word *campanilismo* sums it all up and is suitably impossible to translate into English... the word 'parochialism' doesn't really come near to being loyal to one's village bell.

2

The Property Market

BUYING – WHERE AND WHAT?

Deciding on a location

Deciding where to plant your roots in Italy can be an exciting
and rewarding adventure. The country is richly diverse and
every region has its highlights and drawbacks. There are many
considerations, but the obvious starting point is the amount of
capital you have available. In general, the most expensive
properties are in and around the major cities of the north; on the
shores of the northern lakes; along the Ligurian coast; in and
around the coastal resorts of Amalfi, Sorrento and Capri; and
also along the Costa Esmeralda in Sardinia. Tuscany has now
happily joined the league, partly due to the number of properties
bought by foreigners, with an ever-extending wave of new boom
areas. However, the price of property varies greatly, and general
rules are hard to formulate. The cost of a town-centre apartment
is likely to be comparable to the equivalent in the UK, whilst a
ruined barn may still cost considerably less. Once you have lost
your heart to a particular region, it is advisable to rent an
apartment or house, preferably at different times of the year, to
experience the seasonal climate changes and to give you a
working base whilst searching for your dream.

HOUSING OPTIONS

Keeping up with the neighbours

In the second half of the twentieth century, standards of living in Italy dramatically changed. Less than sixty years ago, living conditions in many Italian homes were still very basic, particularly in rural districts, where many homes were without bathrooms or indoor lavatories. Since then, the Italians have more than made up for their poor past, and houses and apartments have been restored, built and furnished to luxury standards that would put the average British house to shame. The home in Italy, like one's car and clothes, is now a prestige symbol, and no expense is spared.

Housing styles

In keeping with the general diversity of the country, there are many categories of property in Italy. The typical large Italian family living in one unit is fast becoming a legend. With the birth rate on the decline, modern housing, especially in the large northern cities, is adapting to accommodate the nuclear family with one or two children. In rural areas and the less industrial south, it is still quite usual to find two, three or even four generations cohabiting in apparent harmony. The continuing depopulation of the many hamlets and villages due to unemployment and the mechanisation of agriculture has left many rural properties to fall into ruin. Wealthy Italians are beginning to show more interest in renovating a country retreat, but foreign buyers, mainly northern Europeans, remain the answer to most country estate agents' dreams.

Old rural houses

At the bottom of the housing market in Italy are the many rural houses, of differing dimensions, that were gradually abandoned during the post-1945 era, and which now lie slowly deteriorating deep in the country. They are often far more that 100 years old and can be located in the most beautiful surroundings.

Unfortunately they are usually in very inaccessible places, and there may not be a road at all for one or more kilometres. Houses of this type are constructed in stone, usually locally quarried, and roofed with terracotta pantiles in the south, and stone or slate in the north. The interior typically has floors of brick, roughly plastered walls and a beam and brick ceiling.

The ground floor is generally dark, gloomy and damp. It would have been used for animals or for making wine and does not connect with the living space upstairs, to which, in southern and central regions, there is usually an external staircase. The living area usually has a large central fireplace, which would have been used for both cooking and heating. The property may or may not have a bathroom, running water and electricity, depending on when it was last lived in. Obviously, conditions vary considerably from houses that need to be rebuilt totally to those that need only superficial restoration.

Old urban houses

The urban population was always somewhat wealthier than the rural one and old town houses are large and elegant. It was very common for one extremely big building, a *palazzo*, to be constructed in the form of numerous large apartments, with a communal hall and stairway, and in some cases an internal courtyard or garden. The apartments themselves often have high ceilings decorated with plaster moulding and frescoes, and numerous large rooms, usually organised in a circular pattern, so that it is possible to move from room to room, eventually arriving back at the starting point. As these buildings have never been abandoned to the extent of those in the country, the basics of a bathroom – water, electricity and gas – usually exist. This type of building has often been modified and modernised from time to time throughout its history.

New houses

In recent years, the most prestigious housing has been the 'villa', a house set in the countryside or the suburbs of a town, with a garden. Built to luxury standards internally, villas unfortunately often have rather ugly, or at least bland, exteriors of pastel-painted cement. They seem to have little in common with the housing of the past, or of the local region, except that the basement or ground floor is not generally a living space. Italians still prefer to live on the first floor, using the *cantina* on the ground floor to park cars and store junk. Terracotta floors have given way to high-fired ceramic tiles, parquet or composite marble. Walls and ceilings are neatly plastered and painted, very rarely wallpapered, and most homes have two bathrooms, usually clad in a flashy show of ceramic tiles. Many homes also have two kitchens, as entertaining and family parties are an important part of Italian living, and part of the house, either an attic, or an adjoining annexe where there is a large dining area and a kitchen, is reserved solely for this purpose.

Condominiums

In the last forty years, many Italians have chosen to live in condominiums, apartment blocks which contain at least five separately owned flats which share facilities and services. The *condominio* (condominium) is run by an *amministratore* (administrator) who is elected by an *assemblea condominiale* (condominium assembly) which comprises individual proprietors. Each member of the *assemblea condominiale* has the power to vote for or against decisions involving the condominium. The power of the vote depends on the milecesimale, the fraction of thousandths which is calculated according to the size of your flat and the number of balconies it has. Ultimately, however, decisions are made by the Italian law which has formulated a very complicated regolamento (set of rules), and you will find your *condominio* probably has a set of *regolamento* in line with the current legislation.

Service charges and maintenance fees are among the most important economic factors in living in a condominium. All bills, apart from gas, electricity and water, are divided between the condominium according to the *milecesimale* assigned to each proprietor. The parts of the condominium for which you are responsible as a community are as follows:

- land on which building stands
- foundations of building
- exterior walls
- roof
- solar panels
- stairs
- entrance ways
- porches
- courtyards.

Residents of a condominium are also usually responsible for the following:

- lift or escalator
- water pump, cistern, pipes
- gas installation
- heating installation (when centralised)
- TV installation (when centralised)
- intercom or videointercom
- waste pipes.

All these can add up to hefty and unpredictable charges. The charges are usually payable in two instalments per annum. An approximation is made for the year and divided in two. But, if an unforeseen maintenance job is necessary, the second instalment can be a nasty shock. Another idiosyncracy of living in a condominium is the heating system. If your condominium has a communal heating boiler then you will find that you will only be able to use your heating in the official heating times which run from October to April, and that the temperature may not be very responsive to the different seasonal conditions.

Housing – useful terms

Appartamento	Apartment or flat in a block or divided house
Monolocale	Studio apartment or bed-sit flat. One room, usually with separate bathroom
Bilocale	Apartment or flat with two rooms, usually with separate bathroom
Casa	House or home – a very general description applicable to any property
Casa Canonica	Old house once pertaining to the church
Casa Gemella	Semi-detached house
Casa Padronale	Country house belonging to land-owner
Casale	Farmhouse or collection of farm buildings
Casetta	Small house
Castello	Castle
Palazzo	Palace, mansion or, most frequently, block of flats or other very large building
Rustico	Rustic or rural property in need of restoration.
Rovina	Ruin – usually in the historical sense.
Villa	Detached house with surrounding area, courtyard or garden.
Villino	Cottage or small house with garden.

REGION BY REGION

Choosing your region

The following property guide may help you in making your decision as to where to settle in Italy. It lists all twenty of Italy's regions in alphabetical order. A few facts about each region are followed by a general introduction to the region's geographical features, economy and property trends.

Abruzzo

Area	10,974 km^2
Population	1,235,060
Inhabitants per km^2	114
Regional capital	L'Aquila
Provincial capitals	L'Aquila, Chieti, Pescara, Teramo
Airports	Pescara, Rome

The Abruzzo region is predominantly hilly and mountainous, being dominated by the Central Appennines which have peaks of up to 2,912 m. Due to the severity of the terrain, the road network is fairly tortuous, with the good roads centering on L'Aquila. There is also a motorway which crosses the region, running inland from Pescara to Rome. Most of the region's commerce and its tourist industry is focused on Pescara, although there are a growing number of visitors who are attracted to the Abruzzo National Park in the mountainous heart of the region, for walking during the summer and skiing in winter.

Other industry in the Abruzzo is concentrated on the processing of the local agricultural products, namely grains and cereals, but even agriculture is limited due to the poor soils and steep terrain, and much of the upland area is given over to sheep grazing. Cheese made from sheep's milk is an important and delicious Abruzzo product. On the more gentle slopes, vines and olives are grown, while along the coast, potatoes are cultivated, and in the valleys around L'Aquila there is saffron, a product that has been cultivated there since ancient times.

The local architecture is typified by roughly built stone houses with small windows, huddled next to each other on hillsides, while the towns tend to be dominated by rather severe stone *palazzi*.

It is not a popular area, either as a holiday resort or as a place to live, partly due to its inaccessibility and its rather bleak climate. The winter in the interior is long and cold, with the

25

mountains retaining their snowy peaks well into the summer. The property market is sluggish and you can expect to pay rock-bottom prices for buildings in need of renovation. Prices on the coast are somewhat more competitive.

Basilicata

Area	9,992 km^2
Population	614,522
Inhabitants per km^2	61
Regional capital	Potenza
Provincial capitals	Potenza, Matera
Airports	Naples, Bari, Brindisi

Basilicata is a mountainous region in which only eight per cent of the land is suitable for cultivation. Despite this, 40 per cent of the work-force are involved in agriculture, working on the smallest parcels of land to be found in Italy. Basilicata has long suffered impoverished conditions, and in recent years it has been tied up with the corruption surrounding the now abandoned *mezzogiorno* scheme for financial aid. In addition, recession has hit the region badly, with factory closures, such as the textile industry in Maratea, being common. The production of crafts for tourism is one of the few local industries that shows signs of thriving.

The landscape and local architecture seem to reflect the way of life in the region. Hill villages, many of which are semi-abandoned, are carved into the land and bleached as pale as the surrounding arid soils. The houses are small and many have flat roofs or very shallow pitched roofs with sun-parched terracotta tiles. The region also has a lot of poorly built modern housing blocks, which invariably look unfinished even if they are not.

Basilicata is not a popular tourist destination. Matera, with its sassi, rock-hewn dwellings, attracts coach parties, but it is a region the tourist passes through, with the exception of the very short stretch of coast on the Tyrrhenian Sea where there is some dramatic scenery. Basilicata also touches the coast briefly at the Taranto Gulf on the Ionian Sea where the flat coastal plain is densely cultivated, with citrus and peach orchards.

Calabria

Area	$15,080 \text{ km}^2$
Population	2,098,137
Inhabitants per km^2	139
Regional capital	Catanzaro
Provincial capitals	Catanzaro, Cosenza
Airports	Reggio di Calabria

Calabria, the toe of Italy's boot, is hemmed in by both a railway line and a coastal road, giving good access to all parts of the coast, but it has little in the way of communications in the mountainous interior, which remains virtually inaccessible. The Sila mountains dominate the northern part of the region and the Aspromonte the south, both rising to heights of almost 2,000 m. The southern part of Calabria has some flat land, and large fertile plains provide grain for the region, but the area amounts to less than nine per cent of the total region.

Agriculture is on the decline, although the coasts are still thickly covered with olive groves and citrus orchards, some of which grow bergamot, a product that is exclusive to Calabria. Ugly industrial developments have appeared at many coastal spots, such as Vibo Valentia Marina, Catanzaro Marina and Crotone. Even so, unemployment is high and the income per head is the lowest in Italy. Calabria has always been impoverished, and the tough conditions in the region gave rise to mass emigration in the 1960s and 1970s.

Tourism is one aspect of the Calabrian economy that is on the upturn. There are many fine spots along its extensive coastline although, apart from the headland at Tropea, there is always the railway and road to cross. Generally, new coastal properties are not built to the same standard as in other regions and may make undesirable investments. The coast was never inhabited much in the past due to its vulnerability to attack, so almost the only old buildings you will see are defensive coastal towers. However, the hinterland holds many attractive old hill villages built of a greyish colour stone with terracotta roofs.

Campania

Area	13,595 km^2
Population	5,563,230
Inhabitants per km^2	409
Regional capital	Naples
Provincial capitals	Naples, Avellino, Benevento, Caserta, Salerno
Airports	Naples

Just under a quarter of Campania's population lives in and around Naples, which is choked by industrial developments, as is Salerno. Despite the dominance of industry, agriculture, especially the cultivation of tomatoes, is also an important element of the local economy, employing as it does 24 per cent of the workforce, although agricultural salaries are well below the national average. In contrast to the poverty of agricultural workers, there are the wealthy hotel owners and restaurateurs who are based in the luxurious tourist resorts, including Amalfi and Sorrento, as well as the offshore island of Capri. The local architecture reflects this state of affairs, with small, semi-abandoned stone villages in the steeply rolling hills, and immaculately painted villas and *palazzi* in the resorts along the coast. There is also a good deal of very poor architecture, particularly on the fringes of the main cities, where there is tower after tower of shoddily built apartment blocks.

Property both in Naples and on the prestigious Campanian coast is a valuable asset.

Emilia-Romagna

Area	22,122 km^2
Population	3,952,304
Inhabitants per km^2	179
Regional capital	Bologna
Provincial capitals	Bologna, Ferrara, Forli, Modena, Parma, Piacenza, Ravenna, Reggio nell'Emilia
Airports	Rimini, Ravenna, Forli, Bologna

Emilia Romagna is a flat, intensely cultivated region with at least half of the land given over to large-scale farming. It is Italy's number one producer of grain, sugar beet and fruits such as apricot, cherry and peach. It is also important for the cultivation of tomatoes, vines and rice. The flat, monotonous landscape is criss-crossed by numerous major rivers including the Po. Many of the rivers empty into the Adriatic where the flat Emilia-Romagna coast is edged by sandy beaches and extensive areas of reclaimed land.

The region is also well endowed with industry, having many large towns with even larger industrial outskirts. These towns mostly have attractive historic centres, with arcaded streets and brick *palazzi* centreing on the ubiquitous cobbled piazza and its neatly restored cathedral. Country properties tend to be prestigious estates with neat red-roofed farmhouses. Many farms are involved in the production of cheeses, cured hams and salamis which are well known throughout Italy, while Parma claims international fame for its ham and parmesan.

Emilia-Romagna is a region where people live and work but strive to escape from in the holiday periods. Due to the general affluence of the region, property prices are quite high.

Friuli-Venezia Giulia

Area	7,846 km^2
Population	1,228,180
Inhabitants per km^2	157
Regional capital	Trieste
Provincial capitals	Trieste, Gorizia, Pordenone, Udine
Airports	Venice

The small, semi-autonomous region of Friuli-Venezia Giulia is made up of the snow-capped Alps which form the border with Austria in the north, rolling vine-covered hills in the centre and flat alluvial plains that extend to the Adriatic coast in the south. The mountains, which have peaks well over 2,500 m, provide pasture lands for sheep, while the plains are intensely cultivated with grain and fruit orchards. Industry has built up around all four of the provincial capitals, with a refinery and one of the most important commercial ports on the Adriatic at Trieste, which is within a stone's throw of what was once Yugoslavia.

The coast, dotted with lagoons and marshes, is not a popular tourist destination, with the exception of the resort of Grado, although the mountain resorts attract a certain number of holiday-makers. Generally, the region is avoided because of its cold damp winters. Property is reasonably priced and attractive. Venetian architecture dominates many of the towns. In the mountains there are well-built chalets of stone with slate roofs, and on the coast, particularly on the Lagoon of Murano, you will find traditional fishermen's houses built of reeds with cone-shaped roofs.

Lazio

Area	17,203 km^2
Population	5,056,119
Inhabitants per km^2	294
Regional capital	Rome

Provincial capitals	Rome, Frosinone, Latina, Rieti, Viterbo
Airports	Rome

The region of Lazio has a central position, touching all five regions of central Italy as well as Campania, and it is criss-crossed by a good road network. The countryside is characterised by pretty rolling hills, dotted with gracious villas, stone-walled towns, vineyards and olive groves. There are also a great number of hazelnut orchards, Lazio being the second largest producer of hazelnuts in Italy. Agriculture plays an important role in Lazio's economy despite the growing industry that surrounds Rome and stretches southwards to Latina.

The architecture of Lazio is typified by the many fortified hill towns, which are built of a greyish stone and which contain tall, thin houses. Prices for property in Lazio's hill towns are high; the same is true for property on the palm-lined coast from where Romans either commute or where they have their weekend retreats.

Liguria

Area:	5,415 km^2
Population	1,789,225
Inhabitants per km^2	330
Regional capital	Genoa
Provincial capitals	Genoa, Imperia, La Spezia, Savona
Airports	Genoa, Pisa

Liguria is one of the smallest regions in Italy. It is dominated by the Ligurian Apennines and Maritime Alps which sweep up from the Tyrrhenian leaving only a narrow but very beautiful coastal strip. The coast has been a popular holiday destination ever since the British started coming here in the 1920s.

The Côte d'Azur, which is a continuation of the Ligurian coast, is probably more fashionable nowadays, but the gracious villas and elegant palm-lined promenades which characterise many of the resorts and spots such as Lerici, Rapallo and Portofino are as prestigious as they ever were. The attraction of the region also lies in its all-year-round temperate climate, and the shelter from the cold east winds provided by the mountains.

The architecture along the coast, as well as being typified by turn-of-the-century villas, has many *palazzi* with monochrome painted façades and sometimes *trompe-l'oeil* decorations. The architecture inland and away from the resorts and cities is quite different, with small stone hamlets in the hinterland and fishing villages along the coast, the most spectacular of which are those in the Cinque Terre, one of the steepest and most dramatic coastlands in Italy.

Due to the steepness of the terrain, agriculture is limited. The hills are stacked into almost vertical terraces of olives and vines in places. Liguria is also known for its cultivation of flowers, particularly carnations, which unfortunately means that unsightly greenhouses often mar the view. First and foremost, however, the Ligurian economy is based on industry. Genoa very important port. Savona and La Spezia also have large commercial ports and their own fair share of industry.

The Ligurians are not short of money, although they are sometimes seen by other Italians as the 'most careful' people in the nation. Property is expensively priced, particularly along the coast, where the value of property has soared due to strict building regulations.

Lombardy

Area	23,834 km^2
Population	8,891,318
Inhabitants per km^2	371
Regional capital	Milan
Provincial capitals	Bergamo, Brescia, Como, Cremona, Mantova, Milan, Pavia, Sondrio, Varese
Airports	Milan, Bergamo

The region of Lombardy has a diverse landscape which ranges from the flat alluvial plain of the River Po to the gently rolling hills that gradually rise to the dramatic peaks of the Alps, which shelter Italy's famous northern lakes. Lombardy is also crammed full of art and architecture, stylish shops and high-quality restaurants. It is the wealthiest region in Italy and also the most expensive. Most Lombards would prefer to have nothing to do with the rest of Italy, feeling that it only hinders them.

Wealth is gained not only from industry, which is mainly concentrated around Milan, Brescia, Pavia and Varese, but also from agriculture. The soils of the Po valley are rich and well-watered and yield a wide range of high-density and quality crops through the use of modern farming methods.

One of the negative aspects of the region is its climate. Although the northern lakes and the Alps enjoy a dry climate, elsewhere it is very often damp and foggy. Winter arrives early and summer is stiflingly hot and humid.

To uplift the spirits in times of gloomy weather, the Lombards drink *grappa* (spirit) often flavoured with myrtle. The further north you travel in Lombardy the more you will also find other additions to the diet such as German beer, black sausages and wurstel, while *polenta* (maize flour) is one of the basic staple foods throughout Lombardy.

Property in Lombardy, like everything else, is very expensive, exclusively so around the northern lakes, where luxurious villas are set in luscious gardens. Property in the capital, Milan, is also fairly prohibitively priced.

The Marches

Area	9,694 km^2
Population	1,420,829
Inhabitants per km^2	146
Regional capital	Ancona
Provincial capitals	Ancona, Ascoli Piceno, Macerata,

	Pesaro, Urbino
Airports	Ancona, Rimini

The Marches is one of the most underrated regions in Italy. It is characterised by a splendid landscape, mostly hilly or mountainous, which is dotted with charming hill towns and villages, many of which are reminiscent of Tuscany. The Marches also enjoys a long stretch of the Adriatic coast which is edged by flat, sandy beaches all the way, with the exception of the Conero, a headland that rises to a height of 572 m.

Unfortunately, along the coast there is a railway and a motorway to contend with, as well as some hideous coastal developments. Excellent fish restaurants partly compensate and there are some delightful coves and places to reach by boat off the Conero. The Conero is also a centre of red wine-making, while excellent white wine, Verdicchio, is made around Jesi and Matelica.

The local economy has improved greatly over the last decade, with the development of new industries and the use of modern farming techniques to cultivate cereals and grains, as well as fruit along the coast. Some of the traditional industries of the region are shoe-making at Civitanova, paper-making at Fabriano and majolica ceramic making at Pesaro and Urbino. Other main centres of industry are Ancona, Pesaro and Falconara Marittima, where there is a large petrochemical works.

The local architecture is typified by gracious *palazzi* built of small bricks in the towns, while stone farms and farm-workers' houses dot the countryside. The numerous villages also have some surprisingly dignified architecture as well as picturesque narrow streets. The property market in the Marches is still relatively behind the times and it is possible to find very cheap properties that are in need of renovation. Often, however, such properties are virtually inaccessible, without roads or any services.

Molise

Area	4,438 km^2
Population	331,670
Inhabitants per km^2	75
Regional capital	Campobasso
Provincial capitals	Campobasso, Isernia
Airports	Pescara, Naples, Foggia

The region of Molise is where north and south Italy meet. There is the orderliness of the north but also the poverty of the south. The region is more fertile and better-watered than regions further south, having a well-forested landscape and many wide river valleys which are intensely cultivated with grains, cereals and potatoes. Areas of coastal plain bordering the Adriatic are also cultivated. Most of the terrain, however, is too steep for farming. The Matese mountains, which belong to the Apennine chain, are the highest point of the region, with peaks reaching up to 2,050 m. The mountains are used for sheep-rearing which, with agriculture, is the main form of income in the region.

Industry has not really developed very much, except around Termoli. Traditional cottage industries include knife-making at Campobasso and Frosonone, and bell-founding at Agnone. The poor economy of the region is not helped by the frequent occurrence of earthquakes which have devastated many towns. Isernia, the capital of the province, still bears the scars of the earthquake of 1984, and even now whole sections of the town are propped up with stout wooden scaffolding.

Property in Molise is not rated very highly, and the region is not popular either as a holiday destination or as a place to live.

Piedmont

Area	25,399 km^2
Population	4,431,064
Inhabitants per km^2	174

Regional capital	Turin
Provincial capitals	Alessandria, Asti, Cuneo, Novara, Vercelli, Turin
Airports	Turin, Milan

Piedmont shares the northern character of neighbouring Lombardy, but the region is generally less expensive and has better wines and food. Like Lombardy, Piedmont is over-towered by the Alps, although it has fewer lakes, and has vast flat plains surrounding the Po. Piedmont also has a delightful region of hills, south of the Po, known as the Langhe. Asti Spumante and Cinzano originated from here, as do some of Italy's most prestigious red wines. The Langhe boasts a number of charming wine-making châteaux and is an area that is particularly popular with British and Dutch holiday-makers.

Agriculture in Piedmont is wide-ranging, although one of the more important crops is rice. Piedmont's industry, centred on Turin, is largely based on car manufacturing, with Fiat leading the way. More traditional Piedmont industries include the production of wool. In the vicinity of Biella, old and often abandoned wool mills line the river valleys. Textiles, particularly artificial fibre, continue to be important, and it is here that much of the clothing for Italy's fashion industry is produced.

The architecture in Piedmont is as varied as the landscape. In the mountainous regions there are many small hamlets where the houses are built of grey stone and have either slate or stone-tiled roofs. In the flatter fertile regions, there are elegant villas dating from the eighteenth and nineteenth centuries with red roofs and surrounding parklands. As it is a wealthy region, many well-built and professionally designed modern buildings are in evidence.

Puglia

Area	19,347 km^2
Population	3,946,871

Inhabitants per km^2	204
Regional capital	Bari
Provincial capitals	Bari, Brindisi, Foggia, Lecce, Taranto
Airports	Bari, Brindisi, Foggia

The region of Puglia is relatively flat apart from a range of gently undulating hills, the Murge, along the Ionian coast and a splendid rocky peninsula, the Gargano, which juts out into the Adriatic. Although the coast is not mountainous only 34 per cent is made up of sandy beaches, most of which are to be found along the Adriatic coast. The coastline is otherwise rocky, with low red cliffs along the Ionian.

Despite a chronic shortage of water, with only two major rivers and a very low annual rainfall, the Puglian economy is largely dependent on agriculture. The land is covered by mile after mile of olive groves, many containing a giant variety of the olive tree, and endless vineyards. The vines on the Salentine peninsula, the heel of Italy's boot, are particularly noted, both as table grapes and for wine. In the north of the region, the great plain known as the Tavoliere around Foggia produces three-fifths of Italy's durum wheat, the essential ingredient of pasta.

Puglia also has a fair amount of industry. At Taranto there is an iron and steel works, at Barletta cement manufacturers and at Brindisi a petrochemicals plant. Taranto and Brindisi are also important ports, the latter being the main point of embarkation for Greece. The cities of Puglia rate with the roughest and toughest in Italy. Crime is commonplace, and the threat of the Mafia is ever-present. With the exception of Lecce, which has some outstanding Baroque architecture, the cities of Puglia are probably best avoided.

By contrast, the countryside and the property in it are very attractive. Rural Puglia is reminiscent of southern Greece, being littered with neatly whitewashed, little cube-shaped houses that are draped with bougainvillaea and other flowering climbers. Puglia is also the region of *trulli* houses, unusual cone-shaped dwellings built of stone, now a major tourist attraction. It has become quite fashionable to buy a *trulli* and restore it as a holiday home.

The price of property in Puglia is fairly reasonable. In Bari, the capital of the region, property has dropped in value over the last year and there has been a decrease in the number of buyers.

Sardinia

Area	24,089 km^2
Population	1,617,265
Inhabitants per km^2	67
Regional capital	Cagliari
Provincial capitals	Cagliari, Nuoro, Oristano, Sassari
Airports	Alghero, Cagliari, Olbia

Sardinia, the second largest island in the Mediterranean, is the most sparsely populated region of Italy. The landscape is harsh, the soils barren and the coasts are either rocky or marshy. There are some 400,000 hectares of woods, among which are extensive forests of cork trees, which provide an exciting splash of colour. The Campidano, a vast plain between Cagliari and Oristano, provides at least some fertile land. Agriculture elsewhere on the island is restricted to the cultivation of vines and olives.

The south-west used to be a centre of mining, but the industry has virtually ground to a halt now, leaving mineheads and slag heaps to scar the land. New industries in Sardinia include petrochemicals at Cagliari and Porto Torres; the latter also has a large plastics industry.

Otherwise the economy is based on sheep rearing. Sardinian *pecorino* (sheep's cheese) is among the best in Italy, while the sheep's wool is used in the weaving of textiles for tourism. Tourism is one of Sardinia's more prosperous industries. It is becoming an increasingly popular destination with Italians for the August holiday, as even in peak season quiet beaches and clean seas can still be found.

It was the Ahga Khan who first introduced tourism to the island in the 1960s when he bought up a stretch of coast, now known as the Costa Smeralda. The resorts and villages developed here are for millionaires only, and life here is a shocking contrast to the rest of the island. New holiday homes built elsewhere along the coast often try to copy the Costa Smeralda look which, apart from being expensive, is meant to appear 'hand-made'. Building specifications often include top-quality terracotta, travertine, handmade ceramic tiles and chestnut beams. Elsewhere on the island, the architecture is very simple, with stone shepherds' crofts in the mountains and simple fishermen's houses on the coast. Town architecture tends to be rather dour and, unlike other Italian towns, few in Sardinia have piazzas.

Most people who have visited Sardinia, including D. H. Lawrence, come to the conclusion that it is a place for holidays rather than long-term stays. The wet, cold winters and the lack of employment prospects are factors against settling down here.

The Costa Smeraldo is beyond most budgets; Alghero, the other principal and only long-established resort on the island is also pricey. Alghero, however, is a place that most people, particularly the British, fly to on a package holiday.

Sicily

Area	25,708 km^2
Population	5,006,684
Inhabitants per km^2	195
Regional capital	Palermo
Provincial capitals	Agrigento, Caltanissetta, Catania, Enna, Messina, Palermo, Ragusa, Syracuse, Trapani
Airports	Palermo, Catania, Trapani

Sicily, the largest and most densely populated island in the Mediterranean, is no longer a holiday-maker's paradise. The coast is littered with shabby resorts and industry. Added to this, nearly all the towns and cities have slum-like outskirts, the worst of which are at Palermo and Catania. The attractions of Sicily lie hidden in its grime and disorder, which often conceal a wealth of art treasures and ancient sites.

From ancient Roman times up until the last decade, Sicily was dependent on agriculture, particularly the production of grain. It is still the major producer in Italy of durum wheat, but industry has reared its ugly head with unsightly petrol refineries, chemical and plastics factories, and cement works on the coast at Augusta Siracusa, Gela, Porto Empedocle and Milazzo. Palermo and Catania are also major industrial centres.

The countryside, despite being parched most of the year round, is surprisingly green, with eucalyptus, citrus and olive trees in abundance. Prickly pear cactus and vines are also profuse. The landscape is mostly hilly, with eroded gullies, ridges and wide open views being typical features.

Architecture in Sicily is flavoured with a touch of Arabic, many of the smaller towns comprising cube-shaped houses with flat roofs. In the hilly regions, houses are stacked higgledy-piggledy, and most towns and villages have a weather-beaten Baroque church. Modern developments have a similar sense of disorder, but without the charm. Many modern buildings lie unfinished and most are flimsily built.

Property in Sicily is undesirable mainly due to the Mafia problems. However, Palermo has led the way in an open protest against Mafia control, and sales have since gradually increased. Prices have also been gradually climbing up with a prospect of a period of stability in the future and a steady increase in the value of city-centre properties.

Trentino-Alto Adige

Area	6,213 km^2
Population	13,613
Inhabitants per km^2	122
Regional capitals	Bolzano, Trento
Airports	Milan, Venice, Verona

Trentino-Alto Adige is made up of two autonomous provinces: Trentino, the capital of which is Trento, and Alto Adige, whose capital is Bolzano. The region as a whole has been granted semi-autonomy since 1948. The Alto Adige region is dominated by the Alps, which divide Italy from Austria. Until 1918 the region was part of the Austro-Hungarian Empire. German is widely spoken and there is still a good deal of Austrian influence, both in the local food and architecture.

Decorative towers, multi-coloured slates, very steeply pitched roofs and Baroque cupolas are just some features of the local town architecture. In the mountains, local architecture is typified by the small chalets known as *baite*, and their larger counterparts, which are built of wood and white-painted stone, with overhanging slate roofs and dark-wood balconies. In the more gentle, hilly areas there are numerous fine estates and many *castelli* (castles), with neat red roofs and turrets.

The region is best known for its skiing facilities which are among the most modern in Italy. The economy, however, is also based on a certain amount of agriculture, with dairy farming and fruit growing (apples and pears) being very common.

Although the province of Trentino is very mountainous, it has many rivers and valleys, including that of the Adige. Agriculture is similar to that of Alto Adige, while the dense forests also provide raw material for industries that use wood. As in Alto Adige, however, tourism is of prime importance.

There is a lot of property for holiday-makers in the region of Trentino-Alto Adige. Therefore, settling down in the region means contending with the holiday resort atmosphere. You can be fairly sure, however, of making a good investment and buying a well-built and designed property.

Tuscany

Area	22,992 km^2
Population	3,581,291
Inhabitants per km^2	156
Regional capital	Florence
Provincial capitals	Arezzo, Grosseto, Florence, Livorno, Lucca, Massa-Carrara, Pisa, Pistoia, Siena
Airports	Florence, Pisa, Rome, Perugia

Central Tuscany with its hill towns, art treasures, vineyards and cypress trees is a delightful area. Other areas of Tuscany are quite diverse. The wide and fertile valley of the river Arno which flows through Florence and Pisa before emptying into the Tyrrhenian coast, is intensely cultivated, with market gardens and flower-growing. The north of the region has the Apennines, the foothills of which, known as the Garfagnana, are thickly wooded.

The Tuscan coast is also varied. The northern part is backed by the jagged peaks of the Apuan Alps which are quarried for marble. The south, by contrast is completely flat, with lagoons, marshes and sandy beaches backed by pine forests.

Tuscan architecture is typified by the stone farmhouse set on a hill, with a token cypress tree, olive orchard and vineyard. The stone of the region is warm-coloured as are the rich terracotta roofs. To add to the general glow there are many fine villas and *palazzi* painted in traditional Tuscan red. On a less grand scale, but nonetheless attractive, are the farmworkers' houses dotted around the countryside and the lovely stone-built towns, where the windows and doors are often arched, and where the *palazzi* are interspersed with numerous medieval towers.

Property in central Tuscany, along with that around the northern lakes, is the most expensive in Italy. The British have swarmed to this area in their hoards, buying up barns for conversion when failing to procure the classic Tuscan farmhouse. British housing agents deal with the British market as much as possible, although you will pay above the odds for this privilege.

The most expensive properties are those that are within a 30 km radius of Florence, Siena or Pisa. Old properties, which are the most in demand, are expected to continue increasing in value. If you are determined to have a Tuscan farmhouse but have a limited budget, areas further afield such as to the north of Lucca and around Arezzo may be worth considering.

Areas to avoid in Tuscany are those built up with industry, namely the industrial belt that stretches along the Arno from Florence to Prato, Pistoia and Lucca. There is also some unsightly industrial development on the coast at Livorno where there is a petrol refinery and at Orbetello where minerals are extracted. Properties on the coast are mostly holiday homes: settling here all year round involves sitting out a cold windswept winter when the resorts are completely dead.

Umbria

Area	8,456 km^2
Population	813,507
Inhabitants per km^2	96
Regional capital	Perugia
Provincial capitals	Perugia, Terni
Airports	Perugia, Ancona, Rome

Situated in the very centre of the country, Umbria is known in the tourist brochures as the green heart of Italy. It is a generally mountainous and somewhat inaccessible region containing the

Central Apennines, although there are no peaks higher than 1,500 m, and the landscape is made up of gentle hills. The undeniable greenness of Umbria is partly because the region is yet to be ravaged by man and partly because it is well-watered by natural sources, rivers and lakes, among the most popular of which is Lake Trasimeno.

Among the hills there are several large flat basins, such as those around Gubbio, Terni and Nocera, and also wide river valleys, the largest of which carries the Tiber between Perugia and Spoleto. These flat areas are cultivated with grain, while the surrounding hills are covered in olive groves and vineyards. Industry, which is fast eating into the flatter areas of the region, is concentrated around Terni, Foligno, Perugia and Narni.

Umbrian architecture is sombre but attractive. The stone is lighter in colour than that of Tuscany but the building style is quite similar, with hilltop villages and farming hamlets scattering the landscape, and arches being widely used for windows and doors.

Small and narrow archways set into the walls of houses in Umbria are known as *Porte della Morte* (doors of death). Local folklore says that when there was a death in the house the coffin would be carried out through this opening. Most are bricked up now. Towers are another typical feature: fat, thin, tall and short, sometimes converted into independent living accommodation and sometimes incorporated into a house. You will also notice fine wrought-iron work throughout the region, in the form of balconies, lamp-posts, grills on windows and other architectural features.

The similarities with Tuscany mean that property in Umbria is being brought to the attention of the British buying public as an alternative. In Italy, the region is generally dismissed as a backwater due to the lack of employment prospects. However, local holiday-makers go to Lake Trasimeno, and the Umbrian countryside is gaining popularity with the Romans as a weekend retreat within striking distance of Rome.

Valle d'Aosta

Area	3,262 km^2
Population	113,418
Inhabitants per km^2	35
Regional capital	Aosta
Provincial capital	Aosta
Airports	Milan, Turin

The semi-autonomous region of Valle d'Aosta is officially bilingual, with French and Italian both spoken. The region butts up to the highest of the Alpine peaks that run along the French and Swiss border, including Mont Blanc (4,810 m), the Matterhorn (4,478 m) and Monte Rosa (4,633 m). It also contains the dramatic peak of Monte Paradiso (4,061 m), which is surrounded by a national park.

The region is well endowed with resorts both for summer and winter recreation, the best known of which is Courmayeur. Typical houses of the region are known as *rascards* (chalets built of wood and uncut stone). Properties such as these fetch high prices but are very sturdily built and well-designed. Property in general is more expensive than in equivalent resorts in neighbouring Piedmont, and it is said that the people are somewhat reserved.

Veneto

Area	18,377 km^2
Population	4,361,527
Inhabitants per km^2	237
Regional capital	Venice
Provincial capitals	Belluno, Padua, Rovigo, Treviso, Venice, Verona, Vicenza
Airports	Verona, Venice

The region of Veneto has the eastern Alps in the north and a vast alluvial plain in the south. The plain is formed by numerous rivers, including the Po, that empty into the Adriatic. It is intensely cultivated with cereals and potatoes. Other agricultural products of the region include fruit (pear, apple, peach and cherry), dairy products, and grapes which are grown on the foothills of the Alps. It is also one of the largest growers of sugar beet and tobacco in Italy.

The jewel of Veneto is the beautiful city of Venice. However, there are many other fine towns with distinctive Venetian architecture typified by slender arched windows, balconies and elegant loggias. Many buildings are built of Verona stone which is a warm pink colour, while others are painted with pastel-coloured facades and contrasting dark wooden shutters. The countryside too is well endowed with Venetian architecture, including stately homes and villas.

Venice is said to be the most expensive city in Italy. Property is certainly beyond the average budget. However, it is possible to find rural properties within an hour's drive of Venice at more reasonable prices.

SUMMARY

Whether you choose a tumbledown ruin set in a romantic olive grove, a studio with a view of the sea or a high-tech apartment in a bustling city, it is certain that the search will have been a fast learning curve. Whether your future time in Italy is to be an annual fortnight's holiday or several months at a stretch, it is certain that your initial careful research of the Italian property market will be well rewarded.

CASE STUDY

Sophie and Philip were on the fast track to successful careers in banking. In their mid-thirties, and with no intention of starting a family, they decided to invest some of their hard-earned bonus money into a small property in Italy. Philip, the romantic, yearned for a room with a view – preferably over the rooftops of Florence. Sophie, more pragmatic, imagined finding a purpose-built modern apartment near the Mediterranean. Their frequent but short holidays were devoted to the search. They soon realised that easy airport access was a top priority, and that Italy was a much larger country than they had at first thought, with dramatic climate differences. Weekends at home in their Notting Hill flat soon became devoted to studying maps and books on one subject – Italy. Sophie took a compass and drew circles of a fifty kilometre radius round each of the main international airports. One lucky weekend they flew to Rome and went up to Frascati, staying in a hotel recommended by an Italian work colleague. They were both instantly attracted to the small town poised on one of the Alban hills overlooking the eternal city. Philip was soon exploring the remains of ancient Tusculum and the patrician villas set in magnificent gardens. Sophie was delighted to find that there was not only an excellent bus and train service to the centre of Rome but also easy access to the seaside resort of Ostia, a well-kept Roman secret where the locals enjoy fine seafood restaurants and swimming. That evening, over a bottle of the famous dry, golden wine, they agreed that the only problem that remained was to actually find a flat. Talking later with the hotel proprietor and friend of their Italian colleague, they learnt that his elderly aunt was about to sell her large apartment overlooking the main piazza. The very next morning, the hotelier walked them round to the large Renaissance *palazzo* where his '*zia Luisa*' lived. The moment the shutters were opened and the sun flooded into the lofty living room, Philip and Sophie knew they were going to buy it. With the luck of beginners and minds open to compromise, they had found the perfect solution.

3

The Purchasing Process

SEARCHING FOR A PROPERTY

To begin the search for a property in Italy is to set out on an
adventure. Whether it takes two days or two years, it is possibly
one of the biggest financial commitments that most people make
in a lifetime. It is essential to be aware of the legal procedures,
and there are plenty of bilingual professionals to help you on the
way, especially if you are not very fluent in the Italian language.
Better to enjoy the search than buy in haste and repent at leisure.

Using an agent

In Italy, properties for sale are dealt with by *agenzie immobiliare*
(estate agents), most of which are run on a very small scale.
Many are franchises of nationwide organisations such as
Tecnocasa or Grimaldi, but there is no real chain of estate
agencies, and this makes for a rather parochial service. At worst,
the Italian *agenzia* is a fusty top-floor office, piled high with
folders and pieces of paper, and a sign on the door saying *torno
subito* (back soon). Even at best you are unlikely to come away
with details of properties and photos to muse over at your

leisure. There are still many agencies that do not advertise the price of properties, and agents may be extremely coy about naming a price in the hope that some 'crazy' foreigner will be totally confused and inadvertently offer a great deal more than a property is actually worth. The system tends to be for you to describe the type of property you are looking for, name your price bracket and then follow the agent on a wild goose chase around the area in which you have shown interest. This can be time-consuming and frustrating – especially if the keys have to be hunted down, or the agent has not understood what you are looking for. The local *agenzia* is best consulted when you are looking for regular modern housing or a building plot, because as a general rule they are not accustomed to the hair-brained British in search of a semi-derelict country house to renovate. Fortunately, the increasing necessity for showing properties on websites is producing an improvement in the service (see next section 'Surfing the Internet').

It is worth noting that some British agents try to rake off a commission from both the buyer and the seller at well above the odds. It is for you to decide whether the peace of mind their services offer is worth their fee. The average estate agent's fee is between 2.5 and three percent of the total declared value. If any estate agent asks you to sign a *proposta irrevocabile a aquisito* you should beware the false literal translation it implies. It is not a binding agreement and, within the time limit stipulated, the agent has the right to accept a higher offer from another buyer. It may be an appropriate moment to mention here the delightful Italian saying '*traduttore, traditore*' (translators, traitors). If you are asked to sign a *prenotazione* (a reservation agreement) and pay a holding deposit to the agent you should realise that this is not essential practice. The golden rule at this stage of play is that there is no commitment until the *compromesso* is signed by both buyer and vendor (see later paragraph 'Legalities').

Surfing the Internet

The Internet has become an increasingly useful tool for would-be purchasers of foreign properties. There are several excellent websites offering regional lists of properties for sale. Certainly, navigating through the extensive lists and photos of properties is a pleasant way to spend a dark winter's evening. Most website agents offer bilingual services from the beginning of the search through to finished renovation, and some extend this to sub-letting and maintenance management. They offer an easy path through the daunting bureaucracy of owning a home in Italy. As with any agent, it may be a matter of trial and error until you find one that understands your needs and works professionally towards a successful completion. Many belong to FOPDAC, the Federation of Overseas Property Development, a reputable association of members with experience in the overseas property business. The association undertakes, with its team of lawyers, to look into any complaints you may have with any affiliated agent. The FOPDAC logo is shown clearly on any stationery, and they can be contacted on Tel: 020 8941 5588 or via their website: www.fopdac.com.

Below is a list of some of the most useful online agents:

www.brianfrench.com
www.casatravella.com
www.italiancountryhomes.com
www.italyassist.com
www.italvilla.net
www.lacasaemilia.com
www.lifeinitaly.com
www.romanhomes.com
www.ruralretreats-italy.com
www.themovechannel.com
www.umbriarealestate.com

Searching the media

Other ways of finding property in Italy include searching through the classified advertisements in local newspapers and also in the monthly property journal *Metroquadro* which can be subscribed to on their website: www.metroquadro.com or by contacting them at Metroquadro, via Madonna della Querce 8, 50133 Firenze – Tel: 055 577404. Tecnocasa, a franchise company of more than 500 agents, mostly in northern Italy and in and around Rome, also has an efficient website: www.tecnocasa.com. Rather more prestigious properties are advertised in the monthly glossy magazines such as *Dove, Villa e Casale* or *Case di Class*.

Asking the locals

A final alternative to searching for a property in Italy is to hunt around in the vicinity in which you are interested, especially in rural areas. Someone in the local *comune* or *municipio* (town hall), usually a surveyor or architect, will give you a run-down on local properties that are for sale and may also offer to take you around to see them. A visit to a local *notaio* may also yield a list of properties for sale – some due to inheritance conflict or to an owner dying intestate. Half an hour spent chatting to the locals in the bar or café of most small towns and villages will usually result in being directed to most of the properties for sale in the area you have chosen.

PROPERTY JARGON – useful terms

While searching for a property you are most probably going to have to rely on your Italian, unless you are in British-dominated Tuscany. Your phrase book or pocket dictionary will not get you very far: as with all property markets there is a special jargon. The following is a list of property jargon and vocabulary, while words related to houses and the parts of houses are listed in the glossary at the end of the book:

abitabile	habitable
accessibilita	accessibility
acqua di sorgente	spring water
acquedotto comunale	municipal water system
adatto	suitable for
ammirevole	admirable
agente	agent
ampia metratura	ample size
annessi	attached
antico	antique
a posto	everything in order
arredato	furnished
astenersi agenzie	without an agent
attacate	joined
attrezzata	equipped
belissima	beautiful
ben conservata	well-conserved
ben tenuto	well-maintained
borgo	hamlet
bosco	wood
buona posizione	good position
buono stato	good condition
cancello eletrico	electric gate
caratteristico	typical
casa d'epoca	period house
centralissimo	very central
centro storico	historic centre
circondata da	surrounded by
comodissimo mezzi e negozi	convenient location for public transport and shops
complesso residenziale	residential complex
composto da	composed of
condominio	condominium
consegna	exchange contracts

coppi vecchi	old roof tiles
da restaurare	to be restored
da ricostruire	to be reconstructed
da rifare	to be done
da ristrutturare	to be restored
da sistemare	to be put in order
doppi vetri	double glazing
entroterra	hinterland
facciata	façade
finiture lusso	luxury finish
forno a legna	wood-burning oven
fronte mare	sea-facing
grezzo	uncut stone
ha	hectare
impareggiabile	incomparable
imprendibile	unbelievable
incantevole	charming
in corso di costruzione	in the process of being constructed
in corso di ristrutturazione	in the process of being restored
in parte ristruturrato	partly restored
in ordine	in order
libero	unoccupied
luce	electricity
marmi	marble
mattone	brick
mediatore	agent
metrature	size
metro quadro (mq)	square metre
mutuo compresso	mortgage included
nuova	new
occasione esclusiva	exclusive bargain
oliveto	olive grove
ottime condizione	excellent condition
ottime finiture	excellent finish
ottima posizione	excellent position
ottimo stato	excellent condition

paese	village
paesino	small village
pagamento	payment
pavimenti in cotto	terracotta tiling
perfette condizioni	perfect condition
permutasi con	in exchange with
piccolo	small
pietra-legno originali	original stone and wood
poggio	hill
posto auto	parking space
prenotazione	reservation payment
prestigioso	prestigious
prezzo	price
progetti approvati	approved plans
pronta consegna	ready to exchange contract
proposta irrevocabile d'acquisito	non-binding agreement between agent and vendor
riscaldamento autonomo	independent heating
ristrutturato	restored
rudere	ruin
servizi allacciati	services connected
signorile	distinguished
soffiti a volta	vaulted ceilings
spese agenzia	agent's fees
spiaggia	beach
strada	road
strutturalmente	structurally
subito	straight away
telefono	telephone
termoautonomo	independent thermostat
terreno	land
terreno alberato	land with trees
terreno boschivo	wooded land
terreno circostante	surrounded by land
terreno coltivate	cultivated land
terreno per orto	land for vegetable plot

trattabili	negotiable
trattativa	negotiation
travi di legno	wooden beams
travi a vista	exposed beams
vecchio	old
viale privato	private road
vicino stazione ferroviaria	railway station nearby
vigneto	vineyard
vista mare	sea view
vista monti	mountain view
zona collinare	hilly area
zona tranquilla	peaceful area

THE LEGALITIES

Once you have found the property of your dreams it is time to become pragmatic and employ the professionals who can prevent your dream from becoming a nightmare.

Notaio

You will need to contact a *notaio* (notary), who is the public official responsible for drawing up the *rogito* (deeds) and registering the transfer of property. It is customary for the buyer to choose the *notaio*, unless you are purchasing a flat in a condominium or a plot on a new housing development, as the buyer is usually responsible for paying their fee. They are listed in the *Pagine Gialle* (*Yellow Pages*) www.paginegialle.com under *Notai*. As a foreigner you may well be recommended to one by the agent or the vendor. There is no need to be wary of taking a recommendation as the *notaio* is impartial and acts as a witness for both parties involved. If you do not speak fluent Italian you must have a *scrittura privata* (a simplified version of the contract) read out by the *notaio* and directly translated by a representative or qualified translator. Having read out the *rogito*, the *notaio*, the vendor, and yourself will all sign it.

The *rogito* will consist of :

- description of the property and land for sale
- the date of the sale
- name of the vendor and yourself, the buyer
- the declared value of the property.

Geometra

The first step in the buying process is for the *notaio* to make searches into the ownership of the property in question. This is to ensure the legitimacy of the seller and also to check that there is no mortgage or other payment outstanding. At the same time, the *geometra* is employed to carry out a survey (see the section in Chapter 4, 'The Professionals'). If you are planning to convert or change the property in any way, you should check at this stage with the *geometra* that it is possible (see the section in Chapter 4, 'Regulations'). For example, in some regions, due to limited water supplies, it is not possible to obtain planning permission for a swimming pool.

You will also come up against local building regulations. For instance, unless your house is in a village, you will not get permission to convert a room with a ceiling height of under 2.7m into a living space. Another common scenario is the difficulty in converting a property that is registered as agricultural into a holiday home. If this is the case, you should arrange for the vendor to apply for a de-ruralisation certificate from the local authorities.

The *geometra* should also inform you as to any public rights of way or access on your property. Known as *servitude di passagio*, these rights include access to a well or water source. The rights can be one of two types, either permanent or renewable every twenty years. In the latter case, you can refuse to grant permission when it comes to renewal.

It is also important for the *geometra* to inform you of any public works that are projected, such as roads, electricity lines and so on, that would affect the property. If you are buying a historic building ask the *geometra* to find out if it is listed, in which case there will be restrictions over its use and also its future sale.

If you are buying a property with land, it is vital to check out whether there is any *coltivatore diretto* (farmer's right) to the land. This Italian law enables smallholders to enlarge their farms, by granting them the right to buy any land or building adjacent to their property for a period of up to two years after it has been sold.

The *coltivatore diretto* is only relevant if the neighbouring farmer is willing to pay the price on the drawn-up *rogito*. It has been known for the figure on the rogito to be ludicrously under-declared and the farmer can then step in and buy the unsuspecting new owner out. The *coltivatore diretto* only applies to *casa rurale* (rural property) and legal steps can be taken to avoid the hazard. Your *notaio* arranges for special delivery notices to be given to any neighbouring farmers, asking them to confirm within thirty days whether or not they intend to exercise their rights to the land or building.

In order to qualify for a *cultivatore diretto* you must prove that you earn at least 70 per cent of your income from agriculture or agro-tourism. This has worked to the advantage of some foreign buyers setting up rural bed and breakfast establishments, who then have the same right to buy adjacent properties as they come onto the market and prevent anyone building in close proximity.

Now is also the time, if you are buying a flat in a condominium, to get hold of the condominium rule book, *regolamento di condominio*, to check that you can live according to the conditions set out.

If either the written report of searches or the survey reveal any defects or you have any doubts about the property, it is still possible to withdraw from the proceedings and simply pay the fees for the *notaio* and *geometra* that have so far been incurred. The *geometra*'s fees vary depending on what work is involved in the conveyance.

Compromesso

If you are still happy with the property then the next step is to go ahead with the preliminary contract. While this is being drawn up you should obtain a *Codice Fiscale*, an Italian Fiscal Code number (see the section in Chapter 5, 'Local red tape'). The *Codice Fiscale* will need to be presented at all further meetings with the *notaio*, as well as your passport or identity card. You will also need a *Codice Fiscale* in order to open a bank account, which you will probably be doing in order to transfer money for the purchase (see later section 'Money matters').

Compromesso (the preliminary contract) is a significant commitment and involves the payment of a deposit towards the property as an act of goodwill. The purpose of the *compromesso* is to clarify all the conditions of the sale, including the price and terms of payment.

It is an old practice to declare a lower price on the contract than that actually paid in order to avoid registration tax on behalf of the buyer and income tax on behalf of the seller. Whether you choose to do this or not, you should remember that you too will be liable to pay tax when you come to sell on the property. You should also note that it will be considered highly suspicious should you declare a price that is actually lower than the minimum statutory value according to the *catatasto* (local land registry). There is more information on this in the later section in this chapter, 'Money matters'.

It is very important that the buyer does not sign the *compromesso* until he is perfectly happy with everything written in the contract. Remember that the buyer is in a position to impose conditions or restrictions on the vendor at this stage. Buyers should also be sure that if they are buying a property with a mortgage it is clearly stated that the purchase will only be completed subject to the confirmation from the mortgage or housing loan company that the sums owing are cleared. Once the *compromesso* has been signed there is no going back on the terms.

The signing of the *compromesso*, which involves both the vendor and the buyer or their power of attorneys must take place in the presence of the *notaio*. At the time of signing, the buyer must pay a deposit of between 10 and 30 per cent of the sale price. If the buyer does not go through with the purchase after signing the *compromesso*, they will lose the deposit that has been paid and may be sued by the vendor. If, however, the deal does not proceed because of the vendor, then the buyer has the right to demand up to twice the amount of the deposit paid in compensation. In this case the buyer may not only be able to claim damages, but may also have the sale compulsorily completed by court order.

If there is any doubt in the mind of either the buyer or the vendor as to the final completion of the sale, it is possible to state in the *compromesso* that the deposit is a *caparra penitenziale* (withdrawable). This will prevent any further legal proceedings or claims for damage. However, in the case of the buyer's breaking the contract, he or she will still have to lose the deposit to the vendor, and in the case of the vendor's withdrawing, he or she will still have to pay double the deposit amount to the buyer.

On the other hand, if both the buyer and the vendor want a quick sale and have no differences concerning conditions, price or otherwise, it is possible to have the actual transfer of the property written into the *compromesso*. The only formality required after this is for the document to be officially registered.

Atto

The *atto*, is the final act, when the *notaio* witnesses the transfer of title from one party to another and collects the taxes due on the transaction. With all parties present he will identify them, one by one, and then read through the *rogito* (completion document) in detail, making sure that everyone understands what is being bought and sold. He will need proof that taxes and dues have been paid, and he has to have a *visure ipotecarie* to prove what, if any, mortgages or debts burden the property. With all in agreement, the *notaio* will ask each party to sign before he signs and adds his official stamp to the document. In the case of the absence of either one of the parties he will certify the signature of the *procura speciale* (power of attorney). It is at completion that you, as the buyer, must pay the remaining balance of the price of the property, plus the taxes and *notaio* fees. The vendor must also pay his taxes.

Once the transaction has been completed, the *notaio* will register the new title, within twenty-one days, at the *catasto* (land registry). If you have taken a mortgage he will also register the mortgage deed. It may be some weeks, therefore, before you actually receive your copy of the registered title deed.

If, after inspecting your property, you find that it does not meet the stipulations on the contract or that there are some undisclosed defects, the buyer should contact the seller within eight days of signing the *atto*. If it is necessary to take court action, legal proceedings must be started within one year of signing the *atto*.

MONEY MATTERS

Taxation

The first tax you will pay having bought a property in Italy is the *Imposta di Registro*, a registration or purchase tax. As a second homeowner you are liable to pay 11 per cent of the declared price of the property and 18 per cent on agricultural land.

If you are considering taking up full-time residency in Italy and you can establish residency within a year of the purchase of the property you are then entitled to claim purchase tax at the lower rate of 4 per cent. Apart from the lower property tax, the savings on amenities are also quite considerable, as water, electricity, gas and telephone charges can be up to 50 per cent more for non-residents. However, changing your country of residence is a matter for serious consideration, involving many life changes. The Rome council website www.comune.roma.it has a helpful section listing, in English, the general current requirements for a residence permit.

The *notaio* fees amount to approximately 2.5 per cent of the total declared value. There is also a 1 per cent *bollo* (stamp duty) levied against the declared value.

This declared value is the legal or statutory value placed on the property by the Government, based on the official Land Registry price tables and used to calculate the property tax. It may be considerably less than the actual purchase price and it is this figure that appears on all documents. It follows that the amount of tax payable may be less than it at first appears. This is one of the many occasions that it is wise to take qualified professional guidance.

In the case of the purchase of a property from a private citizen, the buyer must pay a registration impost and a land registry tax. If a property is bought from a company, then *IVA* (VAT) is normally payable instead of the land registry tax. If you are buying a new property, then *IVA* is payable on the declared sale price.

Property tax, *Imposta Comunale surgli Immobili*, (*ICI*), is approximately 0.4 per cent–0.7 per cent based on the fiscal value of the property.

If you take out an Italian mortgage a further cost will be passed on to you by your lawyer for registering the change of the lender with the land registry.

Currency and banking

The Euro replaced the much-loved lira as the legal currency of Italy on 1 January 2002. Notes are issued for five, ten, 20, 50, 100, 200 and 500 Euros. One Euro is divided into one hundred cents and the eight denominations of coins vary in colour and thickness according to their values. Coins are of denominations one, two, five, ten, 20 and 50 cents. The Euro quickly gained in strength against the pound sterling and, although fluctuating daily, is taken here as approximately 1.55 Euros to the pound sterling.

Italian bank accounts are available to foreigners whether resident or not, as long as you enter the bank of your choice armed with your *Codice Fiscale*. You will be given a *libretto di assegni* (cheque book) with the facility *incassare un assegno* (to cash cheques) at your local branch. When paying by cheque, a *carta di garanzia* (cheque guarantee card) is essential. For large purchases an *assegno circolare* (bank draft) is the normal requirement.

Choosing which bank is an important and possibly time-consuming part of setting up your new life in Italy. You should make initial enquiries with your UK bank to find out which Italian bank has reciprocal relations with them. For example, National Westminster links to the Italian bank *Credito Italiano*. However, you may not find a convenient local branch in a rural area, in which case it is worth visiting the most conveniently located Italian banks and asking them about their transfer charges and Swift transfer arrangements. Swift transfers should now go directly to local branches rather than through a devious route of head offices in the major cities. If your UK bank cards show the Maestro logo and your new Italian bank also accepts Maestro you should be able to arrange quick and easy transfers by this method.

Italian banks pay a small amount of interest on credit current accounts, usually between two and three per cent.

Bank charges are generally higher than in the UK and it is tempting to keep your fund in Italy as low as possible however, it is vital not to run into overdraft. There are often unexpected charges levied, including those for each cheque written. Any standing orders for services, such as gas, water, electricity and telephone, may automatically be adjusted after their bi-annual meter readings (see the section in Chapter 5, 'Getting connected'). Beware issuing *un assegno a vuoto* (bouncing cheque), even accidentally, as it can lead to complicated legal problems and result in being barred from ever enjoying the privilege of holding an Italian bank account again.

Online banking is an alternative solution with international banks such as Citibank or HSBC and the facility to transfer funds 24 hours and seven days a week.

Loans and mortgages

Mutui (loans), *ipoteche* (mortgages) for buying property and *mutuo per ristrutturazione* for properties needing restoration can be arranged through an Italian bank or a credit company with varying *tasso fisso* (fixed rates) or *tasso variabile* (variable interest rates), obviously depending on your financial status and eligibility. In general, Italian lenders assess eligibility by the applicant's ability to service the loan and not by potential rental income from the property. An example as a guideline is that 35 per cent of the prospective borrower's net income should cover existing outgoings and the monthly repayments on the Italian loan. If you are self-employed, your income is assessed as the average of the last three years' net income. In this case, rental and investment income will also be given consideration. If employed, then the loan will be based on current payslips and amounts credited monthly to your bank account. Outgoings taken into account are all liabilities, such as UK mortgage or rent, personal loans and any maintenance commitments. All mortgages should be fully repaid by the age of 70 and life cover is required. A mortgage is registered in the *Registro delle Ipoteche* (mortgage register) and charges are made for both registration and cancellation.

In order to apply for an Italian mortgage you will need to supply the following information:

- full address of property
- draft sale agreement of property
- photocopy of identity document

- photocopy of last tax return
- photocopy of *Codice Fiscale*
- *certificato di residenza* – available from *comune*
- survey report by registered surveyor
- *stato di famiglia* – available from *comune.*

Another type of credit that is usually on offer for short term only is the *Cambiali*, a form of I.O.U., which is registered as *cambiale ipotecaria*, where the beneficiary is not guaranteed by a mortgage but, in the case of default, by the debtor's assets. General terms are on advances of up to 75 per cent of the purchase price or renovation costs, with terms of 15, 20 or 25 years.

You may agree to buy property that is already mortgaged, in which case you will be expected to take it over on purchase. It is most important to find out exactly what mortgage payments remain to be paid in order to deduct them from the purchase price. Obviously the services of reputable professionals must be used as the loan scene in Italy is as complicated as that of the UK.

It would be extremely unlikely for a British-based building society or bank to advance a loan on a property in Italy, but many people mortgage or re-mortgage their UK home to finance the purchase. It is also possible, and perhaps simpler, to take out a loan with a British-owned building society or bank. The Woolwich usually offer mortgages of up to 80 per cent of the value of property and Abbey National often go to 85 per cent. Both have offices in Italy and many years of experience in arranging mortgages for UK citizens buying property in Italy. The Woolwich Bank has a customer helpline, in the UK, Tel: 020 8298 4400 for preliminary enquiries. Both banks will readily advise you on the requirements for applying for an Italian mortgage and, if you have not already had a survey carried out, they will arrange to do so for a set fee.

The mortgage contract is usually completed at the same time as the *atto* (final purchase). The purchaser, vendor and *notaio* and probably a representative from the mortgage company will be present. Once it is signed, the mortgage contract must be registered at the *Registro delle Ipoteche* (mortgage register) and the 11 per cent registration tax paid.

Useful addresses
www.propertyfinance4less.com
www.abbeynationaloffshore.com
www.woolwich.co.uk
www.bancawoolwich.it

Banca Woolwich SpA, via Pantano 13, 20122 Milano	Tel: 02 584881
Woolwich Europe Ltd, 30 Erith Hoad, Bexley Heath, Kent, DA7 6BP	Tel: 020 82984771
Abbey National Mutui SpA, via Nicola Putignani 137, 70122 Bari	Tel: 080 5237030
Abbey National Mutui SpA, via Quarenghi 36, 24122, Bergamo	Tel: 03 5313130
Abbey National Mutui SpA, via Marconi 71, 40122 Bologna	Tel: 05 14210028
Abbey National Mutui SpA, viale G. Matteotti, 33, 50121 Firenze	Tel: 055 5001514
Abbey National Mutui SpA, via G. Fara 27, 20124 Milano	Tel: 02 6672906
Abbey National Mutui SpA, via Medina 41/42, 80133 Napoli	Tel: 081 2520038
Abbey National Mutui SpA, via Aaltinate 8, 35139 Padova	Tel: 04 98761380
Abbey National Mutui SpA, via Cicerone 58, 00198 Roma	Tel: 06 328061
Abbey National Mutui SpA, via San Tommaso 24, 10121 Torino	Tel: 011 542000

Insurance

As soon as you complete the contract for buying your property in Italy you will need to cover the building, and the contents once they are in place. You may be recommended to an insurance company by your estate agent or *geometra*, but it is advisable to make two or three comparisons of quotes and terms of claims before committing. It is important to find a policy that suits you, as once it is signed you are generally obliged to renew it annually for ten years. If you wish to withdraw from an insurance policy it is necessary to give six months' notice. The basic insurance only covers *incendio ed altri danni ai beni* (fire and damage). For an added premium you can have cover against *furto* (theft) added to the policy, but check the small print, as payments on claims are reduced by 50 per cent or more if your property does not meet the requirements of security outlined in the policy, such as bars on windows less than three metres from the ground. Most policies work on a *franchigia* basis, which means that a flat cost is deducted from the compensation. Otherwise you get a percentage in return, with a maximum usually stated. If you are in an earthquake zone you should be aware that most policies exclude earthquake damage. Another common problem is the amount of time that your home may be left unoccupied.

INSURANCE BROKERS – useful terms

Below is a vocabulary list that will help you in talking to insurance brokers and reading up on the small print.

acqua condotta	water piping
apparcchiature	appliances
arredamento	furnishings
assicurato	insured party
assicurazione	insurance
assicurazione contro i terzi	third-party insurance

atti vandalici	vandalisation
azione del fulmine	lightning damage
bang sonico	sonic boom
buffera	storm
caduta di aeromobili	aeroplane crash
contenuto dell'abitazione	house contents
contraente	contracting party
cose rubate	stolen goods
danni a terzi	damage to third party
danni eletrici	electrical damages
danno	damage
denuncia	statement
dolo	fraud
esplosione	explosion
fulmine	lightning
fuoriuscita di liquidi	leakage of liquids
furto	theft
grandine	hailstorms
guasti	breaking and entry
incendio	fire
indennizzo	compensation
mobilio	furniture
oggetti pregiati	valuable objects
oggetti preziosi	precious objects
pagamento	payment
perdita delle pigioni	loss of rent
polizza globale abitazione	global policy for house
polizza globale fabbricati	global policy for building
premio	premium
rimborso	reimbursement
riparazione	repair
risarcimento	compensation
rischio	risk
rottura	breakage
rottura accidentale delle lastre	accidental breakage of window-panes

scippo	theft bag-snatching
scoppio	explosion
sinistri	accidents
sommosse	uprising
spargiamento d'acqua	water explosion
spese	expenses
sviluppo di gas/fumo/vapori	gas/smoke/fume leak
tempeste	tempest
trombe d'aria	whirlwind
tumulti	riot
uragani	hurricane
urto di veicoli stradali	crash from road vehicle
valore	value
vento	wind

It may be more convenient to use one of the UK-based or international insurance companies who specialise in covering holiday homes. The website www.schofields.ltd.uk is a useful first point of reference. The UK-based insurer Andrew Copeland International Ltd have a typical comprehensive cover in plain English wording. All premiums and claims are paid in sterling and there are some valuable benefits that you might not get from local Italian policies. Important liabilities such as tenants (if you let the property it is essential to include this), subsidence, landslide and earthquake damage should all be adequately covered. You may also want to be covered for emergency travel to the property to sort out a claim, should it occur whilst you are in the UK. As an example: a policy for a property valued at £60,000 with a contents cover of £10,000 would cost approximately £220.00 per annum, and should guarantee you peace of mind.

SUMMARY

Once you have found a property, you should make sure that you really know what you are taking on before making any commitments. The first point to take into consideration is the location. A property that looks idyllic in the summer months may be buried beneath snow, flooded by a river or blocked from the sun all winter. It may be inaccessible in bad weather and it may also be difficult to heat, especially if there is a problem with the damp.

Next, you need to consider the amenities. Is there a road, electricity and water? Find out how many metres it is to the nearest mains electricity and water source. The cost of connecting these services, roads included, is usually priced per metre and will be an expense that you will need to take into consideration before agreeing to the selling price.

You should also take into consideration the cost of restoration if it is necessary. Unless you are prepared to do the work yourself, you will pay a considerable sum for builders. You will also find that building materials, particularly wood, are more expensive in Italy than in the UK. So do not be fooled into thinking that a low purchase price will translate into a low restoration price.

In fact, one of the reasons that derelict rural property is cheap in some parts of Italy is that it is recognised that the restoration is prohibitively expensive and therefore the property is less desirable and saleable. This is partly why Italians show little interest in derelict properties, preferring to invest their money in building a new villa. Building afresh with modern building materials is somewhat cheaper than knocking down and rebuilding (for more on this see Chapter 4, 'Makeovers').

Buying a property in Italy does not necessarily have to be a traumatic experience. Once you have understood the unfamiliar conveyancing procedures and found the right professionals, the path may be long and convoluted but it should lead smoothly to a satisfactory completion.

CASE STUDY

Pam and David, both professional people in their fifties, had long shared the dream of owning a home in rural Italy. When the youngest of their three children had finished university they decided the time had finally arrived for them to be able to finance the reality. Having studied Italian at evening classes for four years and spent many happy holidays in Umbria, they felt confident and pleasantly excited. Staying in a small *pensione*, they began by trawling the local estate agents in Perugia and smaller towns around. Eventually they met an estate agent who seemed to understand what they were looking for and met them half-way with their efforts in speaking Italian. After viewing several properties that nearly met their expectations, their patience was finally rewarded when they found a small, stone house on a south-facing hillside near Cortona. The roof was sound, water and electricity were connected and the short drive led directly to a tarmac lane. There were some interesting original features and a well-maintained terracotta paving on the first floor. The whole was in need of internal decoration and Pam decided she would definitely want to replace the bathroom and extend the kitchen into an adjoining pigsty. Their evening class Italian had improved rapidly over the weeks of their search but Piero Justini, the owner of the property, spoke in a strong dialect, and there was considerable confusion every time they talked about converting the pigsty. David was worried that Piero resented their plans to change the cottage. At this point, the agent realised that negotiations were seriously falling apart and arranged for a professional translator to accompany them on their next visit to the cottage. Pam and David finally understood that Piero was asking if they would buy his pig. That evening, over a rewarding dinner in the local *trattoria*, Pam and David drank a toast to the translator. Two months passed by whilst searches were made into the ownership and division of land, and planning consent was granted for the conversion of the pigsty. Pam and David finally signed the *compromesso* and committed

70

to buying the cottage – without adopting the pig.

Pam and David now escape to their hillside haven more and more frequently and have made many friends in the locality – both Italian and English. At dinner parties with the latter, when property horror stories are the main subject of conversation, Pam and David raise their glasses again to toast the luck that brought them an efficient agent, a qualified translator and a dream cottage in the area they love.

4

Home Makeovers

The day has finally dawned and you are the proud owner of a home in Italy. Whether it is a modern apartment in a palazzo or a romantic mill deep in the countryside, now is the time when you will want to make it your own. The British are renowned home-improvers and gardeners; their DIY skills are surely now added to the image of the mad dog going out in the midday sun. Before you begin to pull down walls and rip out plumbing and electricity, why not sit in the sun and reflect a while. You are in Italy and remember, when in Rome it is often advisable to do as the Romans.

THE PROFESSIONALS

Architetto

The *architetto* (architect) is at the top of the chain of professionals that you may wish to employ in the renovation of your new home. An architect will oversee the entire project, which means making plans from reconstruction to furnishings, and includes getting estimates and being regularly on site to direct the work. It is needless to mention that it almost always costs more than you expect. The initial *preventivi* (estimates) are often pleasingly low, but there is inevitably an unseen problem lying ahead of any sizeable project. To be on the safe side, it would be realistic to add a further 15–20 per cent on top of the first figure quoted. Renovation estimates are almost always for building work alone and may not include finishing costs or even, in some cases, materials. Obviously, the quality of materials, such as tiles or wood finishes, will greatly vary the costs. Arranged stages of payment should also be clearly agreed in the contract. Allow plenty of time to go through the figures with the architect and have every item explained thoroughly.

Alternatively, you may wish to employ an architect just to draw up the necessary plans for projects that have to be approved by the local *comune* (town hall) (see the section 'Regulations' later in this chapter).

Geometra

There is no exact equivalent of the *geometra* in the UK, the nearest being a surveyor. The job of an Italian *geometra* is to draw up plans for existing property, rather than designing something new. This is not to say, however, that the *geometra* does not draw up plans for new projects, but that a *geometra* would not be the person to employ were you to build a house from scratch. If the renovation you are undertaking involves only minor modifications or is the restoration of an old property, you may well wish to continue to employ the *geometra* that you have already met, whilst making the necessary searches involved in the purchase of your property.

As a general rule, the *geometra* tends to be more practical and may have better contacts in the building trade than the architect. Like the architect, the *geometra* can either partake in the entire project from start to finish or can be employed for one function only. He should approach local tradespeople whom he knows to have a good track record and arrange for estimates for your approval. It is worth considering that the lowest quotes may not always be the lowest by the end of the work. Time is an important factor, and the contract for the projected work should include a penalty clause to be enforced if the work extends beyond the agreed finish date. There may have to be some amicable leeway if bad weather conditions prevail or if you have asked for additional work due to the usual unforeseen snags that invariably dog any renovation programme. A fixed rate per hour or a new contract for a fixed cost for extra work is the best solution for these extra works.

REGULATIONS

Getting planning permission

Permissions required for renovation work depend on the exact nature of the work. It is most important that the correct regulations are adhered to, as working without permission can only lead to disaster. It is not unknown for the local *comune* to order a *condono edilizio* (condemned building) notice, and to demand that the new building work be demolished or/and to impose a heavy fine. In the event of reselling your home it will also be vital to have proof of permission for any work carried out. Once again, the *geometra* is the professional to guide you through the process, as different work requires different levels of planning approval. For example, internal improvements, such as the installation of central heating and new doors and windows, require the *geometra* to submit a simple plan of the project to the local council. This is called a D.I.A and must be submitted at least twenty days prior to the commencement of the work. Structural changes, on the other hand, such as roof restoration, foundation or major work on walls, require the *geometra's* plan to be submitted to the department of *Commissione Edilizia*. Approval may easily take two months or even much longer and also incurs a tax of 5 per cent of the restoration costs. If your home is in an earthquake zone, the renovation may require a seismic study.

Registering

Any changes that you make to the use of the land or property of any house must be registered at the *catasto* (land registry). Land and property are strictly classified in terms of use by the local land registry and it is not always easy to achieve alterations. One of the most common changes to property is from an agricultural status to that of residential.

Changing your garden

Making changes to land also needs planning permission in most circumstances. For example, building terraces in your garden, installing a swimming pool or building a new wall will all require planning permission. Small wooden constructions or greenhouses are usually exempt from planning permission. If you live in a place of tourist interest or on a *strada panoramica* (scenic route), it is forbidden to build anything that would restrict the public view. Strictly speaking, this would include planting a tree that would grow to a large height. However, trees are very highly regarded by all Italians and, unless very dangerous, they are usually allowed their place. Indeed, you should never cut down a tree on your land unless it is dead and you can subsequently, by photographic evidence, prove this was the case. Planting a hedge less than 1.5 m from your neighbour's land or casting shadow on your neighbour's land or building is also strictly forbidden.

In town

If your home is in a designated urban area, you will be expected to conform to the local colour scheme used in the painting of external walls. Enquiries should be made to the local *comune* or *municipio* for the range of permissible colours.

VAT payments and reductions

Renovation and conversion is regarded as new building work, so you will be obliged to pay *IVA* (VAT). These improvements will also increase your local *comune* taxes. Before buying any materials for renovation or employing anyone, you should find out whether the project you are undertaking is eligible for *l'abbatimento dell'IVA* (reduced rate of VAT). Ask your local *comune* or *geometra* for advice and then make an official request to the *sindaco* (local mayor) or your *comune* or *municipio*. The letter must be written on *carta semlice* (official lined paper) and can be bought by the sheet from a *tabbaccherie* (tobacconist's).

Final advice

Be very careful to keep any bills paid as they can be used to offset capital gain on a future sale of your property or in the event of valuation on your death. Remember also that any project that requires planning permission should never be started until you have the *licenza* (permit) in your hand, and then you must be quite certain that you can complete the work before the planning permission date expires.

THE BUILDING TRADE

Employing builders, plumbers, electricians and decorators in Italy is a costly business. Before embarking on any major project you may wish to estimate just how much it will cost. Don't listen to workmen or architects who say it will cost *poco* (little), as it very rarely does. It would be more realistic for you to find out the going rates and insist on having a proper estimate for the job. The final bill will probably be reduced if you offer to pay cash without a receipt although bear in mind that this is not legal. If you have work done in this way you may lose out on getting certificates and guarantees which are assets when it comes to selling your property.

The following section is a guide to the professions within the building trade, each of which is listed alphabetically. The Italian for each profession is provided at the start of each section to enable you to locate the relevant people in the *Pagine Giallo* (*Yellow Pages*) if necessary. Note that the telephone numbers supplied in the *Yellow Pages* are generally home numbers, therefore call at mealtimes 12.00–14.00 or after 20.00 to be sure of catching the person you wish to speak to.

Builders

Muratore (builders) and *imprese di costruzione* (construction firms) usually estimate a job price, known as a *forfait*, or a price per square metre, a *misura*, which includes both materials and labour. If the job is impossible to estimate, for example if it is the restoration of a frescoed wall, then a price is charged per hour, a method of payment known as *in economia*. Alternatively, builders may charge a fixed rate per day, in addition to the cost of materials.

Demolition work can also be calculated at a price per square metre according to the material to be demolished, which may, if specified, include removal of the rubble.

Before employing builders you should not only get an estimate for the job, and preferably be shown a property where they have worked before to see the standard of their workmanship, but you should check that they are covered by third-party insurance against accidents.

Carpenters

Falegname (carpenters) usually are very busy artisans so you may have to wait for your requirements to be seen to. DIY and discount stores do now have a selection of standard measure wooden doors, windows and shutters, but most Italians still prefer made to measure woodwork and joinery. Prices vary

77

depending on the quality of the wood. A carpenter may negotiate a fixed price for the complete job or work by the hour, depending on how specialised the work is to be. The main concern is to order well in advance of the time it will be needed in the stage of renovation.

Decorators

Imbanchini (painters, literally translated white-washers) and *decoratore* (decorators) usually estimate the cost of a job on a square metre basis depending on whether it is *verniciatura* (painting) or *carteggiatura* (wall-papering).It is important to establish whether the price quoted includes the cost of materials. They are usually highly skilled and work rapidly once they have made their newspaper hats.

Electricians

Elletricista or *installatore* (electricians) can be hired by the hour or per electrical point installed. Professional electricians should be registered at your local chamber of commerce, or associated to an organised body or union. If an electrician is completely rewiring your house, ask for a certificate for the work done which can be presented when you come to sell your house. If you are building a new house you will need to show this certificate to the town hall in order to get permission for habitation. If your property does not have an earth and/or trip switch, you are obliged by law 46/90 which came into action in 1990, to have an electrician install them. Your insurance cover will also depend on your electrical installation meeting all safety requirements.

Plasterers

Intonacatore (plasterers) usually work on the same terms as builders and decorators (see above). The price depends on the type of finish you require or whether the existing plaster can be renovated or skimmed. There are several 'rustic' finishes and the plasterer should be happy to show you examples. The English idea of 'rustic' is not necessarily what the plasterer has in mind. Smooth finish is usually the most expensive and, generally speaking, the Italian *intonacatore* is king in the world of plasterers.

Plumbers

Idraulico (plumbers) are usually happy to work by the hour, but for a major installation, such as central heating or plumbing a bathroom, you will probably be quoted a price for the whole job. An official certificate should be obtained which can then be shown when it comes to selling your property. The plumber may suggest accompanying you to the local showroom to select bathroom suites etc.

Tilers

Piastrelliste (tilers). Tiling is an art form and there is a greater selection of tiles than any other form of floor covering. The *piastrellista* will either lay tiles that you have already bought or will supply the tiles you request. You may find it is more economical to order through the tiler as he will probably get a builder's discount. Alternatively, you may wish to enquire about *seconda qualita* (second quality) tiles, those that have slight defects. Price per square metre, for walls or floors, depends on the size of the tile – a diagonal arrangement usually costs about ten per cent more for labour and materials due to wastage.

DOING IT YOURSELF

You may be one of those many people who dream of buying a cheap derelict property and renovating it yourself at your leisure.

It is by no means impossible in Italy, but it is certainly more expensive and difficult than in the UK. DIY is not a very popular Italian leisure time activity – most shudder at the thought of even putting up a picture hook. You may find yourself regarded with a mixture of respect and bemused sympathy by your neighbours and friends.

DIY stores are slowly spreading across Italy and can usually be found on the outskirts of larger towns. However, you may find fewer of the handy pre-packaged DIY goods than you might hope, and it will also be more difficult to hire some of the larger equipment necessary. You will have to 'muck along' with the professional builders and try to do things their way, using the materials they use.

The first place to locate in your nearest town is the *edilizia* (the builder's yard), which stocks everything from sacks of cement, sand and roof tiles to bathroom suites, plumbing parts and insulation. Your next most important source is the *ferramenta* (hardware store), which sells household paint, varnishes, tools, nails and often wood trims such as cornices and skirting boards.

With these two basic sources of materials in mind the following section lists what materials are generally available in Italy and how to say them in Italian, which is half your battle done. Information and relevant glossaries are arranged in subject groups and listed alphabetically.

Building and construction

The *edilizia* (builder's yard) is open five days a week and usually Saturday morning too. Sometimes the *edilizia* closes one weekday afternoon – this varies from place to place. Opening hours tend to be similar to those for businesses, usually from 8.30 a.m. to 12.30 p.m. and 3–4 p.m. to 6–7 p.m. Most builders' yards will deliver materials at an extra cost.

If you use a builder's yard regularly, once they get to know you, your purchases will be put on an account. When you take materials on account, that is without having received a till receipt, you should be given a *bolla di consegna* (delivery note) which can be presented to the finance police should you be stopped and asked to prove the validity of the goods.

It is general practice to go to a builder's yard with a clear idea of what you want rather than expecting to be able to browse around. Materials are usually stacked in inaccessible places, not on view to the public. The following is a list of vocabulary that you may find useful both at the builder's yard and the hardware store.

THE BUILDER'S YARD – useful terms

betoniera	cement mixer
blocchi	hollow clay building blocks
cacciavite	screwdriver
calce	lime
canna da fumo	chimney pipe
cartongesso	plasterboard
cazzuola	trowel
cemento	cement
cemento bianco	white cement
chiodi	nails
condotto	duct
coppo	roof tile
filo di ferro	metal wire
frattazzo	float
ganci	hooks
gesso	plaster
ghiaia	gravel
girabecchino	hand drill
isolamento	insulation
lana di vetro	mineral fibre
livello a bolle d'aria	spirit level
malta	smooth cement
martello	hammer
mattoni forati	hollow bricks

mattoni pieni	bricks
mattoni refrettari	refractory bricks
mazza	mallet
morsetto	clamp
pala	shovel
piale	plane
pinze	pincers
polistirene espanso	expansive polystyrene for insulation
polvere	crushed rock
sabbia	sand
scagliola intonaco	slow-setting plaster
sega	saw
seghetto per metalle	metal saw
spatola	spatula
squadra a battente	set square
tasselli	raw-plugs
tavelle	construction blocks
tenaglie	pincers
tondino	reinforcing metal wire
trapano elettrico	electric drill
travi di cemento armato	reinforced concrete beams
umidità di risalita	rising damp
viti	screws

Decoration

In Italy, many households employ decorators rather than
undertaking the general maintenance themselves. The market for
decorating materials is therefore smaller than in the UK and
consequently the selection too is more limited. Colour ranges
are restricted, as are types of paint such as non-drip, and there is
a very small, and also expensive, selection of wallpapers. The
ferramenta (hardware store) will be the source of most of your
materials but not your inspiration, although some ferramenta
will mix colours to your requirements. The *ferramenta* keeps

regular shop hours (8.30–12.30, 5–8), closing one afternoon in the week and also on Saturday afternoons and of course Sundays. The following vocabulary should be of help in getting together your shopping list and asking for the things in the shop itself. For vocabulary for tools and other implements that are also sold in a *ferramenta*, see the previous vocabulary list. Note also that among other things, the *ferramenta* usually cuts keys, and sometimes glass.

THE HARDWARE STORE – useful terms

acqua ragia	white spirit
carta da parati	wallpaper
carta fodera	lining paper
carta lavabile	washable wallpaper
carta tipo vinilico	vinyl wallpaper
carta vetrata	sandpaper
chiodi	nails
colla	glue
filo a piombo	plumb line
forbici	scissors
idropittura	water-resistant emulsion
intonacare	to plaster
nastro di carta adesiva	masking tape
penello	paintbrush
penello ad angolo	radiator brush
penello piatto	flat paintbrush
penello rotondo	round paintbrush
piccone	pick
pittura lavabile	washable emulsion
pitture	paints
raschietto	flat stripping knife
revestimenti murale	wall coverings
rullino premigiunti	seam roller
rullo per verniciare	roller for painting
sega	saw

smalto	gloss paint
spazzola	brush
spazzola metallica	wire brush
spugna	sponge
stucco antico	textured paint
stucco gia pronto	ready-mixed filler
stucco in polvere	filler in powdered form
tampone	paint pad
tempera	non-washable emulsion
tende	blinds
vernice	varnish or gloss paint
vernice antiruggine	anti-rust paint
viti	screws

Electrics

If you are renovating a property that needs completely rewiring you will have to employ an authorised electrician who will supply the certificates and guarantees officially necessary in the event of future sale. The electrician oversees all electrical connections as far as the fuse box, which is the property of ENEL (*Ente Nazionale per l'Energia Elettrica*). ENEL control the amount of electricity that is supplied, the maximum being three kw.

If you want a larger electricity supply than this, you must have another meter installed which, of course, incurs extra expense and rental charges. If you overload your electricity supply, the tripswitch, now obligatory, will intervene. Before flicking the tripswitch back on, remember to turn off one of the appliances that caused it to overload in the first place.

You may want to do minor jobs to do with electricity. You will find materials in a specialist shop, usually called *materiale elettrico*. If you are bringing electrical appliances from the UK, check that they will run on the Italian current, which is 220 volts AC/50 Hertz, and remember that you will need to put Italian plugs on, which are unfused and consist of either two pins or three pins in a single row.

The vocabulary below should help you when purchasing electrical goods and materials, for, as is invariably the case, you will have to ask for what you want at the counter rather than browse around and pick items off a shelf.

ELECTRICAL GOODS – useful terms

apriporta elettrico	electrically operated door
cacciavite	screwdriver
cavo	flex
condutore	conducting wire
connettore	connector
contatore	meter
filo	wire
fusibili	fuses
giunzione	junction
guaino	plastic covering on wire
illuminazione	lighting
interruttori	switches
interruttori automatici	tripswitches
lampadina	light bulb
morsetto	terminal grip
morsetto fermacavo	cord grip
nastro isolante	insulating tape
pinze da elettricista	pliers
pinze spellafili	wire-stripping pincers
presa	socket
presa incassata	recessed socket
scatola	box
spina	plug
termostato	thermostat
terra	earth
tubo di protezione	plastic tubing
tubo flesibile	flexible tubing
tubo rigido	rigid tubing

Flooring

In the eyes of Italians, flooring, in whatever form, is most
definitely a job for the professional. However, if you wish to have
a go on your own, read on. Tiles of all shapes, colours and sizes,
terracotta to high-glazed, are sold at the *edilizia*, builder's yard, or
at one of the many prestigious stores that sell kitchens and
bathrooms.

You will find an enormous selection in the form of display
cards, although only a few tiles will actually be in stock, most
only being available on order. If you are ordering a style that is
not in stock, follow up the initial request regularly to check that
they have been able to get the tiles and that the style you have
chosen has not been discontinued. Promises of arrival a week later
are not always realistic: it is better to place your order at least a
month or so before you actually require it.

Perhaps the next most popular type of flooring is parquet but,
unless you already have experience, you will be undoubtedly
employing someone to lay it. It is generally sold in stores that
specialise in parquet and have a very wide selection to choose
from at a very wide range of prices. The prices depend not only
on the type of wood and the dimension, but the quality of the
grain. *Prima scelta* (first quality) has a completely regular grain;
seconda scelta (second quality) has occasional knots, while *scarto*
(rejects) are irregular in size, grain and texture.

Unfortunately, the expense of parquet is not only in the actual
wood, but also the glue with which to fix it (particularly if you
need the strong glue for larger dimension parquet) and the sealant
and polish.

Wall-to-wall carpet is not a very popular option as a floor
covering in Italy. It is generally sold at pricey interior design
shops that also make blinds and curtains to measure. Pure wool
carpets are generally twice the price of polyesters. Rush matting
is the same price as a polyester carpet. The shop that sells the
carpet will also arrange for a fitter to lay it.

Linoleum is also less common in Italy than it is in the UK. The *ferramenta* often stocks a limited selection, at quite reasonable prices, but if you are looking for cushion-backed lino or something with style, you will have to try a carpet shop.

The following is a list of vocabulary that may be of use when you are selecting a floor covering.

FLOOR COVERING – useful terms

colla	glue
cotto	terracotta
feltro	felt underlay
formato	size/shape
juta naturale	natural backing
juta sintetica	synthetic backing
gomma	vinyl
inchiodata	tacked
lana	wool
largezza	width
linoleum	linoleum
lunghezza	length
malta di sigilla	grout
marmo	marble
moquette	carpet
parquet	parquet
pavimento	floor
posa	laying
rotoli	roll
spessore	thickness
superficie lucida	gloss surface
superficie satinata	matt surface
supporto schiuma	sponge backing

Plumbing

For plumbing materials, your best bet is to go to the *edilizia* (building yard), although for materials related to heating systems, go to the shop that initially sold the boiler or other parts of the system. There are three basic systems used for supply plumbing: plastic, iron and copper, in that order of preference. Copper plumbing is predominantly used with brass pressure joints, although soldering is used in some circumstances. Waste plumbing is done in plastic and in concrete, there being two grades of the plastic tubing, white and orange: the orange is thicker, more durable and also more expensive.

The following vocabulary list should help you in asking for what you need.

PLUMBING MATERIALS – useful terms

box doccia	shower unit
caldaia murale	wall boiler
dado	bolt
fascette	bracket
filettatura	plumbing tape
guarnizione	washer
lavabo	wash-basin
lavello	sink
liquido sgrassante	flux
manicotto	sleeve
piatto doccia	shower base
raccordo	joint
radiatori	radiators
riscaldamento	heating
rubinetto	tap
saldatura	soldering
sifone	U-bend
stagno	solder
tubi di plastica	plastic pipes
tubi di rami	copper pipes
tubi di scarico	wastepipes
tubi zincati	zinc-coated iron pipes
valvola	valve
vasca di bagno	bath tub
vaso igienico	toilet

Woodwork

Woodwork is expensive in Italy, the price of wood being generally higher than in the UK. As much of the wood is imported, prices vary according to the vagaries of the exchange markets. To buy wood you must locate your nearest *legnami* (timber yard). There are generally two types, those that sell *legname da costruzione* (timber for construction) and those that sell *legname da lavoro* (timber to be worked). Timber yards are generally open five days a week and closed at the weekends. They tend to keep office hours, that is having a shorter lunch break than do the shops (8.30–12.30, 2.30–6). For nails, screws and all tools, go to your local *ferramenta* (hardware store).

The following is a vocabulary list that may come in handy when you are buying materials for a woodworking project. Some of the more general tools that you may use are listed under 'The builder's yard' (see above).

THE TIMBER YARD – useful terms

abete	fir/deal
bedano	beveller
blochetto per levigare	sanding block
bullone	bolt
cacciavite	screwdriver
cacciavite con punta stella	philips screwdriver
carta vetrata	sandpaper
grana media/fine	medium/fine grain
castagna	chestnut
cera	wax
cerniere	hinge
chiave	spanner
chiodi	nails
chiodi di calzolaio	tacks
chiodi di ottone	brass nails
colla vinilica per legno	wood glue

compensato	composite board
ganci	hooks
girabecchino	hand drill
impregnate	preservative
lacche poliuretaniche	polyurethane
lama di seghetto	saw blade
legno	wood
levigatrice orbitale	orbital sander
levatrice a nastro	belt sander
levigatura	sanding
listelli	small planks or strips
lucidate	varnished
maniglia	handle
martello	hammer
matita di falegname	carpentry pencil
metro a nastro	tape measure
modanatura	moulding
morsetto serragiunti	clamp
pasta di legno	wood-filler
piallate	planed
piallone	plane
pino	pine
pomelli	knobs
punta	drill bit
quercia	oak
raspa	file
saracco	wood saw
scalpello da legno	wood chisel
sega	saw
sega circolare	band saw
seghetto alternativo	jig saw
serratura	lock
serrature magnetiche	magnetic catches

CASE STUDY

Joanne and Michael Billington led a comfortable life in London.
Joanne ran a successful catering business in the city and Michael
worked as a freelance graphic artist. Their three-year-old twins,
Ruby and Jason, were attending pre-school and Joanne and
Michael juggled looking after them with the help of an au pair.
Their summer holidays were always taken in the same beautiful
villa near Assisi, in the unspoilt region of Le Marche.

One cold January morning, the post arrived with the news that
the villa was not to be available for the next summer as it was
going to be sold. Joanne, rushing out of the door to take the
children to school, hastily left the letter on the kitchen table for
Michael to read. All day she thought of only one thing – how
could they buy the villa? That evening, after the twins were at
last asleep, Michael came into the living room holding the letter.
Joanne looked up and instantly knew that he shared her dream.
They stayed up most of the night planning a completely new
life.

Two years later, their new life was in full swing. The twins
attended the local *scuola materna* and spoke Italian as fluently
as they spoke English. The barns attached to the villa had been
converted to holiday accommodation for residential courses:
Joanne teaching Italian rural cookery with the invaluable help of
Maria from the village and Michael running small groups of art
history tours in and around Assisi.

None of this successful transformation in life style had come
easily. Their first year in Italy had been plagued with problems.
The necessary planning permissions for the conversion of the
barns had seemed interminably long in arriving. Their first DIY
attempts at decoration had come to grief when they found how
difficult it was to buy materials within eighty kilometres of the
villa. The hot weather they had always enjoyed on their summer
holidays had disappeared into the mist of autumn and
plummeted to zero over their first Christmas. Joanne's abiding
memory of that first year was of wearing green wellies from

morning to night. Their first lucky break came when they met a local architect, father of one of the twins' new school friends. He arranged for all the necessary planning permissions to be hurried through and recommended local builders, electricians and plumbers. Somehow, by Italian magic, the building work was completed in time for Joanne and Michael to welcome their first students. From then on life became the dream they had first shared.

5

Settling In

FIRST STEPS

As Italy and Britain are both member countries of the EU,
moving house to Italy should, in principle, be no different from
moving house within the UK. In reality, the move involves a
good deal more organisation. If you are taking up full residence
in Italy there will be a number of odds and ends to tie up before
you leave, on top of the preparation of paperwork for your
arrival in Italy. If your new Italian acquisition is to be a second
residence, then another set of rules apply.

This chapter attempts to make the whole process easier and
deals with how to organise your move, getting ready, and what
you should do on arrival in bureaucratic terms.

Knowing that any move can be a stressful experience, let
alone one involving a possible language barrier, then you may
need to sit down with a glass of wine before you read on.

REMOVALS

Your new home awaits you and now the time has come to make
yet another important decision. Should you start afresh and buy

all your furniture and furnishings, take the route of the professional international removers, or compromise and transport some belongings under your own steam?

By the time you need to make this decision you will probably be quite well acquainted with your local Italian shops. Maybe you have already window shopped and yearn to spend, spend, spend in Italian style. On the other hand, you may have discovered very little that seems worth the exorbitant price tags. There are few secondhand furniture shops in Italy, and old furniture such as pine cupboards and chests of drawers are regarded as antiques and fetch high prices by British standards.

Moving yourself

Anyone who has travelled frequently on the Italian *autostrada* (motorway) will have overtaken an archetypal English registered Volvo estate loaded with the paraphernalia of home contents. It is not an impossible route to take, but it is not always as cheap as it would appear after the costs of crossing the Channel, petrol, tolls and overnight stays are taken into consideration. Self-drive van hire adds extra costs and time restrictions which can affect safety. However, if you are determined, you should have no major difficulties, since the border regulations within the EU have been lifted. If you are bringing furniture over 50 years old from Britain you should apply beforehand for permission from the Italian Ministry of Culture and then declare it on arrival in order to avoid any difficulties in re-exporting it. The address for the Ministry of Culture is:

Ministerio per I Beni e le Attivita Culturali
Via Baudana Vaccolini Costanza 6
00153 Roma
Tel: 06 5810846

Removal companies

If you are taking up full-time residence it will almost certainly be worth getting quotes from a few international removal companies. It is advisable to use one that takes responsibility for all the paperwork involved, which includes writing a full inventory in both English and Italian. Most removal firms also take charge of the packing and unpacking. Any items you elect to pack yourselves may not be covered by their overall insurance against loss or breakage. Insurance premiums will also be increased for any valuable objects that amount to over 20 per cent of the total amount insured. The cost of the removal depends on the volume of your belongings. A typical three bedroom move from the UK to Italy should cost approximately £2,500. However, if two or three households share a container you may be able to save around £600. The problem with sharing a container is waiting for other households in the same area. The most frequent removals are made to northern Italy during the summer. Below are some of the international removal companies in Britain. Other companies can be found by simply looking in the *Yellow Pages*.

Allied Pickfords
Heritage House
345 Southbury Road
Enfield
Middlesex EN1 1UP
Tel: 0800 289229
www.pickfords.co.uk

Crown Worldwide Movers
Kingsbridge Road
Barking
Essex IG11 0BD
Tel: 020 8591 3388
www.crownworldwide.com

Martell's International Removers
Queen's Road
East Grinstead
West Sussex
RH19 1BA
Tel: 01342 321303
www.martells.co.uk

WHAT TO TAKE

Having considered the transportation of your worldly goods, you should now think seriously about exactly what to take with you. Maybe you are already familiar with just what is available in and around your new home. If you have read Chapter 4, 'Home makeovers', you will be well aware of the scarcity of DIY materials and, therefore, may wish to take a supply with you. You could also consider taking flat-pack units, especially if you are installing a kitchen, for although Italian kitchens are attractive, they are pricey. Once an Italian has invested in one, when they move house they often take their kitchen with them.

Fitted carpets, should you want them, are also worth bringing from the UK, both for the competitiveness in price and the quality. Bedding in Italy is beautiful and you can pick up fine, embroidered sheets at local markets as well as very well-made and prettily coloured eiderdowns. However, duvets are not very widely used and cost at least double their UK price, so if you have one, pack it.

As far as electrical appliances go, although they are slightly more expensive, you are probably better off buying them in Italy where they are adapted to run on 220-V and covered by local guarantee. An electric kettle, however, is well worth bringing as the Italians are not a tea-drinking nation and have no use for them: hence, they are scarce and very expensive. If you do pack electrical appliances, then try to bring the sales invoice in case you need to prove that you have paid VAT, although you may still have to pay the difference between Italian VAT and British.

You should note that British TV sets and phones tend not to function properly on the Italian system. Other incompatible appliances are lamps or light fittings which take bayonet bulbs, as only the screw-in type are used in Italy. Plugs are different too, so if you are bringing an appliance with a built-in plug you will need an adaptor.

Unless you enjoy lavishing money on stylish clothes, pack as large a wardrobe as possible. Apart from outdoor markets, cut-price clothing is just not Italian. *Saldi* (sales) take place in January and early February, and also in late July and August before summer vacation begins, but even then you will pay above the odds.

Remember that winter is as cold in Italy as it is in the UK, so include a raincoat and a winter coat if you are planning being in Italy then. If you have a fur coat this may be your chance to wear it. Animal rights campaigners are neither active nor militant in Italy and Italians love wearing fur. Sportswear and sports equipment are also something you should consider bringing with you if you wish to save money.

If you are moving to Italy with your children then, for purposes of economy, make sure they have a good supply of clothing packed too. There is no Italian equivalent to Mothercare, Boots, Early Learning or any of the other reasonably priced chain stores that exist in Britain. Benetton, Prenatal and Chicco are the principal Italian chains, but they are not cheap. If you are travelling with a baby you may wish to pack a supply of favourite foods as the selection is somewhat restricted in Italy, and the Italian diet is very different to the British.

It is a good idea to pack a few of your own favourite foods too as Italians eat Italian and nothing else, so that ingredients for other cuisines are not widely available. Spices and condiments are particularly useful to bring. Cooking utensils are also somewhat different in Italy, and while you will be able to buy superb saucepans and colanders for pasta, you will not find woks or traditional British saucepans with lids and a single handle very commonplace.

If you still have space in your packing, slip in a box or two of tea as it not only makes good gifts but is much more expensive to buy in Italy. Italian tea brands include Winston and Yellow Label, with tea of every flavour from apple to cherry, but you will find little in the way of bulk household tea. Indeed, bulk household anything, apart from wine, pasta and washing powder, is not common. This includes toiletry products which are sold in expensive pharmacies or small boutiques rather than in mass production as on the shelves of stores such as Boots. Body Shop have opened up chains in the major cities. Generally, however, toiletries, cosmetics and pharmaceuticals are cheaper from the UK.

If you take a regular prescribed drug, pack a good supply to give you time to locate its equivalent in Italy. Many drugs are marketed under different names. Your UK doctor or the drug manufacturer should be able to tell you the brand name used in Italy, and whether the formula given in Italy is exactly the same as your current prescription.

TAKING YOUR PET

Nearly all pet owners hate to leave their animals behind, even for short holidays. A permanent move to Italy could be heart breaking, especially for children, if the family pet doesn't come too. Fortunately, the relaxation of the British quarantine law has made it perfectly feasible for UK residents to take their pets back and forth.

Pet passports

The Pet Passport scheme only applies to cats and dogs, and there are a limited number of entry points when returning to the UK. As it can take several months for your pet to qualify for the scheme, it is advisable to contact your veterinary surgeon as soon as possible. Your pet will need a microchip implanted

under the skin of the shoulder and to be vaccinated against
rabies. There will also be a simple monthly blood test after the
vaccination to prove immunity. Your pet should then be ready to
travel but it is always a good idea to check with the Italian
embassy. Regulations can change – for example, as they did
during the Foot and Mouth epidemic – as both cats and dogs can
be carriers without showing symptoms.

Dog owners in Italy are obliged to have their dogs tattooed
with a registration number but the alternative of the microchip
implant is acceptable. Any stray dog found without a tattoo or
microchip implant risks being destroyed. In Italy, dogs are
annually vaccinated against rabies and must have logbooks to
prove that this has been carried out. The pet passport meets this
requirement.

Rabies

Rabies is still apparently prevalent in the most northern parts of
Italy. The other risk that pet owners should be aware of is the
danger from snakes and porcupines, especially in the south. It is
advisable to keep an up-to-date venom antidote in the
refrigerator during the hot summer months. Your local Italian vet
or pharmacist will readily advise you on this.

Pet insurance

Pet insurance is the next item on the list. It is available
separately or as a supplement to your home insurance. Various
policies are obtainable covering veterinary bills and any harm or
damage your pet might cause.

The Department for Environment, Food and Rural Affairs,
DEFRA, have excellent fact sheets on taking your pets out of
the UK, and an informative website www.defra.gov.uk and
helpline Tel: 0870 241710.

LOCAL RED TAPE

Going through any bureaucratic procedure in Italy is a time-consuming and often frustrating business. In the larger cities, long queues and less than helpful staff exacerbate the problem. It is often difficult to make headway without the right personal contacts to make things move along. Many people take their problems to an *agenzia* (agency) which specialises in dealing with bureaucratic formalities. As well as the correct documents, almost any bureaucratic transaction requires *bolli* (official stamps), the most common type of which cost 7.75 Euros and are purchased from the *tabaccherie* (tobacconist's).

Registering with the police

Any visitor to Italy intending to stay for longer than 90 days is required by law to register with the local police, either the *Questura* or the *Commissariato* or the *Stazione di Carabinieri*, within eight days of arrival. If you are staying in a hotel, *pensione* or an approved campsite or other tourist accommodation, this formality will automatically be done for you.

Applying for a permit to stay

A *permesso di soggiorno* (permit to stay) may be issued by the *Ufficio Stranieri* (Foreign Department) or *Questura* in your regional capital. The local police in a small town may be willing to apply for the permit on your behalf. You will be given an application form and required to write a formal letter of request on *carta bollata* (special document paper) which can be purchased from the *tabaccherie*.

The type of permit you apply for will depend on your reason for being in Italy. However, you would normally be requested to present proof of your financial means or, where applicable, your proof of status – i.e. student, worker, property owner, retired person, pensioner or person of independent financial means. The *soggiorno* is free of charge and issued for three months and then renewed for either two or five years. Failure to keep your *soggiorno* in valid date can result in a heavy fine.

The completed application form and your letter with *bollo* attached should be returned to the police with the following documents:

- passport
- photocopy of principal pages of passport
- three passport-sized photographs
- health insurance or Form E111
- *bollo* (official stamp).

You should be the proud owner of your *permesso di soggiorno*, sometimes known as *carta di soggiorno*, within three months.

Non-EU nationals

All non-EU nationals wishing to apply to live permanently in Italy, for whatever reason, should contact the visa section of their local Italian Consulate.

Applying for residency

If you plan to take up residency in Italy, once you have obtained your *permesso di soggiorno*, your next task is to register at the *Ufficio Anagrafe* (Municipal Registry Office) in your nearest *comune* or *municipio* (town hall). Take your *permesso di soggiorno* and passport or identity card and explain that you wish to become a resident of the local *comune*. Once you are a resident you will find it much easier to do domestic transactions such as opening a bank account, buying a car, having electricity connected, etc.

To obtain this certificate simply go to the *Ufficio Anagrafe* where they will issue a print-out with the relevant information. The cost of the print-out is nominal but you may be required to affix a *bollo* so that the Ufficio Anagrafe can then plant their official stamp over it.

Codice fiscale

The *codice fiscale* is a card with your fiscal tax number on it. You will be asked to present this card for any number of transactions, from joining a sports' club to opening a bank account. Registration is surprisingly simple. Find your provincial tax office, known as *Ufficio Imposte Dirette*, and present your passport or identity card. Your *codice fiscale* will be issued there and then so that the Italian tax authorities can begin immediately to collect taxes from you. Your *codice fiscale* card should be carried with you at all times.

Driving licence

If you hold a standard pink EU drivers' licence you are entitled to drive your UK-registered car without any alteration to it. If your UK licence is still the old green type, then you must have it translated. The Italian State Tourist Office, 1 Prince's Street, London, W1R 8AY – Tel: 020 7408 1254, will do this free of charge. Alternatively, it might be a good moment to update to the EU pink type.

If you wish to own and drive an Italian registered vehicle you should, in principle, change your EU licence for an Italian one. You will be required to supply a certificate confirming that you have no current driving offences and this will be available by applying to your local embassy or consulate. In practice, many expats drive around in Italian registered cars carrying international driving licences, but this could lead to problems if you are involved in an accident or claim insurance.

If you need help in applying for an Italian drivers' licence, go to any *agenzia* that advertises *patente* (licences) in their window or to an ACI (Automobile Club Italiano) office. The process is certain to be long and drawn-out and the minimum requirements you will need to provide are the following:

- *certificato medico* (Doctor's certificate) with *bollo* (official stamp)
- stamped and signed licence translation (only for green EU licences)
- original driving licence
- resident's certificate with *bollo* (official stamp)
- three passport-sized photographs (one endorsed)
- *codice fiscale* (tax code card)
- passport or identity card
- *permesso di soggiorno* (permit to stay).

When you have assembled all these important bits of paper it is advisable to photocopy each and every one of them before taking them to your local *motorizzazione* office. Be warned that this particular zone of Italian bureaucracy enjoys a reputation for being unhelpful and long winded. Try to keep your patience and hang on to your photocopies as there may well be an alarming period of time when you will be without any licence at all. The official who relieves you of all your paperwork should give you a receipt and cover letter entitling you to drive in the meantime.

Once you are the proud owner of your new *patente* (Italian drivers' licence) you are legally required to carry it, along with your *libretto* (car documents), car insurance and passport whenever you are driving.

Useful websites

www.idl-international.com	international driving licence information
www.britain.it	British Embassy in Rome
www.embitaly.org.uk	Italian Embassy in London
www.noiitaliani.com	Italian Consulate London
www.theaa.com	Automobile Association
www.aci.it	Automobile Club d'Italia

GETTING CONNECTED

Moving into a new home will most probably require having various services connected. The *allacciato* (connection) of gas, electricity and telephone for properties without these facilities will be an expensive and possibly long procedure. The further the property is from the nearest mains or telephone line the greater the cost. Once connected you will then be billed for these services six times a year. The easiest way to pay is to arrange a direct debit from your bank account, especially if you are not in full-time residence. There are standing charges for each of the services, and failure to pay a bill by the due date will result in immediate disconnection. Reconnection is costly and often very long-winded to arrange. Alternatively, you can pay the bills at the post office or over the counter at your bank, paying a small handling charge.

This section deals with each of the basic services, describing the procedures involved, from getting connected to paying bills. You should keep receipts of all bills paid and also the official declarations that are given for any installations or modifications that are made. Information is also provided as to the different heating options available so that you can best decide how to heat your home during the winter.

Electricity

ENEL (*Ente Nazionale per l'Energia Elettrica*) is the national electricity board, although there are also private companies now in operation, particularly within the industrial sector in northern Italy where hydroelectric power is available. Domestic supply, however, is generally dealt with by ENEL who oversee the following:

● bringing the electricity supply to a property
● the installation, connection and reading of meters
● increasing or decreasing the power supply.

To find the local head office, look under ENEL in your local telephone directory, but if you are having electricity connected you will need to go to the office itself to open a contract. First telephone to find out their opening hours (they are invariably closed in the afternoon) and also the documents you will need to take, although generally the following are required:

● passport or identity card
● *codice fiscale*
● *certificato di residenza*
● last meter reading.

The contract, among other things, will state the amount of power at your disposal and whether you are resident or not. Note that non-residents pay considerably higher rates. Within a short time, an ENEL employee will come to your home to do the necessary work. Once the meter is turning there is nothing more to do other than wait for your first bill.

Bills are issued every two months and are calculated according to an estimated consumption rather than an actual one. Your bill will also include standing charges, tax and costs for any work you have done by ENEL. A bill based on your real consumption, known as a *conguaglio* is issued twice yearly.

Should you be in credit you will receive the difference through the post in the form of a postal order which can be cashed at the post office.

Gas

If your home in Italy is in an urban area you will most probably be connected to or have access to *metano citta* (town gas). If you want to be connected to *metano*, the first step is to locate your local office by looking in the *Pagine Gialle* (*Yellow Pages*) under *Gas Esercizio*. Telephone the office, find out their opening hours and also the documents needed in order to be connected. Normal documents required are:

● *stato di famiglia*
● *certificato di residenza*
● *dichiarazione sostitutiva dell'atto notorieta*
● *codice fiscale.*

All these documents with the exception of your *codice fiscale* (tax code number) are available from the *Ufficio Anagrafe* at your local *comune* or *municipio* (town hall). The third document in the above list is a standardised declaration of your good character.

With these documents in hand, go to the *metano citta* office and complete the appropriate forms. The two basic forms are:

● *richiesta esecuzione lavori e/o fornitura gas* (request to have work done and/or gas supplied);
● *domanda di fornitura e/o allaciamento* (demand for supply and/or connection)

Once your meter is turning, the next formality is to pay your bill. A *metano citta* employee will deliver your *fattura* (bill) every two months. Like electricity, the bill is calculated according to an estimated consumption rather than an actual consumption, with a *conguaglio* (reckoning-up bill) every six months.

Telephone

If you want to install or connect a telephone you will need to contact the national telephone company SIP (*Società Italiana per l'Esercizio delle Telecomunicazioni*). This can be done over the phone by dialling the number 182 and requesting whichever of the three services below that you require:

- *trasloco* (moving)
- *subentro* (taking over a telephone)
- *nuovo impianto* (new installation).

In addition to your request, you will have to supply your name and address. Your request will probably be followed up by an acknowledgment through the post which will tell you the date by which the work should be carried out and also give you a reference number that should be kept for further communications.

If you are having a new telephone installed, a SIP technician will come to your home; however, the connection may not be made until a week or so later. The connection and other services are made by telephone communication which means that SIP will call you when the work is completed and supply new clients with their telephone number.

When your phone is connected, the dialling tone will sound '*tu-tuuu*'; when you dial a number you will hear a ringing sound '*tuuu*' repeated at intervals. The continuous sound '*tu-tu-tu*' means the number is engaged. The charges made for using the telephone depend on the time of day and the distance.

Telephone bills are sent every two months and are calculated on the number of *scatti* (meter points) you consume. You will also pay a regular rental charge and tax.

Heating options

The way you heat your home will depend largely on whether you live in an urban or rural area. Urban properties, as mentioned above, usually have access to town gas, and this is probably the most economic way to run central heating. If you do not have access to town gas, economic alternatives include installing a *serbatoi* (gas tank) which will be filled directly from a lorry when necessary. There are usually several competing gas companies in an area, so you should shop around for estimates and also services before settling on any one. Many companies offer to give an estimate and assess where best to install the tank free of charge.

Regulations concerning the positioning of a gas tank stipulate that it must be at least 7 metres from any houses and 15 metres from public buildings. Competitive gas companies offer the actual tank free of charge (although it remains the company's property), and only bill the client for the gas that is delivered. To find gas companies, look out for billboards along the roadsides in your locality or consult the *Pagine Gialle* (*Yellow Pages*), looking under *Gas Compressi e Liquefatti*.

If your property will not accommodate a gas tank and you live in or near a mountainous or forested area, you may consider using wood as your fuel. Italian rural homes often have a radiator inserted at the back of their fireplace which heats other radiators in the house and may even provide hot water. It is a good system but one that depends on keeping a fire alight.

Oil and electricity are both too highly priced to consider as economic forms of regular heating. Other alternatives include running gas fires from *bombola* (bottle gas). Bottle gas comes in cylinders of varying sizes, although the most common is the 40 kg. The same gas companies that supply gas tanks often sell gas bottles too. Terms of delivery and deposits paid on bottles may vary from company to company, but the gas itself is sold at a fixed price, which is not particularly cheap, and so is not a very good solution to regular heating.

CASE STUDY

Judy and Richard, newly retired and ready for a new life, had bought a light and airy apartment in Rapallo on the Mediterranean. The day they received the letter from the *notaio* confirming that the completion had been successfully made by proxy was a day of celebration. Their house in West Sussex was already sold and they had just two months before moving.

The next day, Judy, who had just retired from a long career of teaching, drew up a long list of things to do which closely resembled a school timetable. Richard, a retired bank manager, began phoning around for removal quotes and storage costs. Difficult decisions had to be made over sentimental baggage and a vast library of books. At the weekend, their adult children came to stay and happily relieved their parents of almost half their worldly goods. Judy and Richard were looking forward to buying some furniture that they had already selected in a store in Rapallo and which suited their modern apartment. On the Sunday evening, after the children had left, Judy and Richard sat down to write a finalised inventory. A certain amount of bargaining ensued between them – Judy agreeing to allow Richard to take his fishing gear if she could take her exercise bike, and both of them accepting that they should have a very large car boot sale.

During the next week they had three removal companies visit to quote for their big move. Two were large international names and the third, a local family firm who happened to specialise in international home removals. They were both equally impressed with the family firm, who not only gave a detailed description of exactly how they would pack but also supplied an informative leaflet on all the steps involved. A date was agreed and the days rushed past in a series of farewell parties and last minute chores.

Two months later, sitting on their balcony on their brand

new Italian loungers, looking down on the sparkling blue Mediterranean, Judy and Richard complimented themselves on their good choice. The removal company had not only delivered everything intact and on time, but had also made the move a cheerful and completely stress-free affair.

6

Letting Property

When your Italian home is finally finished from the roof to the garlic crusher, you may decide to recoup some of your expenditure by letting it out to holiday makers – at least while you are not there. Certainly it would seem to be a logical conclusion if your property is destined to lie empty for months on end. The school holidays, especially the long summer months, are the prime dates when rental prices reach an optimum. The only obvious exception is a chalet or apartment in a ski resort when Christmas and the February half-term dates will command high rates. Rates will always depend on the standard of comfort or luxury you offer and the location. A grand Tuscan villa with a swimming pool or a luxurious apartment in a *palazzo* on the Grand Canal in Venice will reach dizzy heights in rental income. The more typical rural farmhouse offering good family accommodation is always well sought after and a swimming pool can more than double the rental price in the heat of summer.

PROS AND CONS

The temptation of raking in high summer rents should not lead you to overlook the negative side and the hidden costs of holiday letting. Not everybody can cope with the idea of allowing strangers into their home in their absence. In any case, you should allow sufficient time before the tenants arrive to pack away your personal belongings and sentimental treasures. Keeping a small room or safe cupboard especially for this purpose is the easiest solution. Even with the very best of tenants, there will always be a certain amount of wear and tear to furnishings. If you are unlucky enough to have a booking from the holiday makers from hell, then you may find they can wreak damage in ways beyond belief. Your only consolation will be that the pre-arranged security or damage deposit covers any nasty costs. Your own home insurance policy can and should be extended to cover tenants' damage and their personal safety.

GOING IT ALONE

If you decide to undertake the letting of your home without the help of an agent you will need to draw up comprehensive details including photographs of your property. If you wish to make specific stipulations, e.g. no pets, no smoking, etc., this is the time to mention it. You may also consider it worth stating that owner access should not be unreasonably denied at any time in case of maintenance or other problems. A helpful guide to the general running of your home, the domestic appliances and, if applicable, the cleaning of the pool, will be as advantageous to you as it will be to your tenants. Spend time on collating useful local information and nearby tourist attractions, and don't forget to list emergency numbers, doctors, dentist and the nearest hospital. The more helpful information you provide, the fewer questions you will be asked and the more at home your guests will feel. The object is to create a dream holiday that your tenants will want to repeat. Offering discounts for advance bookings for the following year may well save you future advertising costs. A simple booking form, in any case, is an absolute essential, an example of which is shown below.

WEBSITE ADVERTISING

Creating a website is an increasingly popular means of offering a virtual tour of your home and the local area, with links to airlines and ferries making it the easiest way to arrange a holiday. Web creator companies such as Oneandone.co.uk are a good starting point unless you have the technical expertise. Access to up-to-date availability and booking online are significant factors in increasing bookings. If you want to accept payment by credit card online, it may be worth surfing the net for companies who undertake this service. There are also a number of online companies who offer you a webpage on their site for advertising holiday properties, and many of them give free introductory or trial offers.

ADVERTISING IN NEWSPAPERS AND PERIODICALS

If you begin to advertise in a national newspaper shortly after Christmas when people are recovering from their festive spending and looking ahead to some welcome sunshine, a small ad. may well be sufficient to fill your high season weeks. *The Sunday Times* have a large section on self-catering holidays in Italy and offer four consecutive weeks of lineage ads for the price of three. Close inspection of the columns will help you word your advertisement to catch the eye. The busy telesales staff on 020 7782 7799 are often helpful when you finally get through the obligatory musak waiting time. You can ask them to quote a price for the words you have ready and then insist that the lines be filled. Rather than pay for an expensive white space at the end of a line you may want to add in a superlative or descriptive adjective or two. Only the first word is offered in bold type and this is usually the place name. As the advertisement is already under the Italy column you may want to begin with the region. If you decide later in the year that you have a few weeks free for letting you can always try an ad. mentioning the fact that the property is available due to cancellation and this usually brings results.

HANDLING ENQUIRIES

Answering calls or emails, sending out brochures and booking forms, acknowledging cheques and monitoring availability can all be very time-consuming. Holidaymakers may become very reliant on a friendly voice and may ring to ask anything from whether you have an ironing board or a coffee machine to exact details of the route. Your patience may be strained, but it is probably worthwhile giving a friendly reply to someone who is going to stay in your home.

MAKING IT PAY

When you calculate the profit you hope to make the following costs should be estimated and deducted from the grand total of rental income:

- advertising
- printing brochures, booking forms and stationery
- cleaning and maintenance
- service bills
- wear and tear
- supplementary expenses, e.g. tenants telephone and heating
- void weeks
- telephone, Internet and postal costs for handling bookings
- insurance
- income tax on rent revenue.

If you have Italian residency and you want to let your Italian home for more than a few weeks a year, you may wish to visit the website agriturismo.com. Similar to that of the better known French gîte holidays, Agriturismo helps and offers grants to owners of rural properties who wish to offer farmhouse holidays, bed and breakfast or simple country cottage accommodation.

KEEPING IT LEGAL

If you are resident in the UK, obviously you must declare any income from your property. If you have taken up Italian residency then, again, the income must be declared, but bills for certain repairs may be set against the tax levied.

Holiday rentals, meaning terms of less than three months, are not subject to the Italian rent act known as *equo canone*. You can, therefore, draw up a contract to suit your requirements. Keep it as simple as possible but demanding an advance deposit of up to 50 per cent of the rent and a refundable damage deposit are essential starting points. The remaining rent should always be paid before the tenants take possession. The deposit should be held until the property has been checked after the tenant's departure. Service bills, electricity, gas and water, are usually costed into the rental price, but the telephone bill is often a point of dissension. Beware tenants who insist that they will only be using their mobile phones. If you do leave the phone for the tenant's use, then request an itemised bill for the relevant dates and deduct the amount from the deposit. Ask your tenant to wait for the return of their damage deposit until the bill has arrived, and then provide a copy of the appropriate section of the bill as proof of their calls made. Then you only have to hope that their deposit covers the bill – or that they are decent enough to make up the difference! If all this seems too awful to contemplate you may wish to employ a helping hand. Most areas have an expat who eeks out a living by looking after other expat's properties in their absence.

BOOKING FORM 200-

NAME ....

ADDRESS...
....
....

POSTCODE ....

TEL/FAX ....

email:...

Number in party .... (maximum ?)

Ages of children ....(special requests? e.g. cot)

Dates required ....
(Saturday to Saturday)

Signed ....

Date ....

(Tick as appropriate)
Bed linen and towels (not swimming) are provided
Villa cleaned before arrivals
Extra cleaning, cooking and baby-sitting available
at extra cost and by arrangement
Fridge filled for arrival by arrangement

Telephone and PC/Internet connection by arrangement
Heating in winter months supplement by agreement
Sorry, no animals allowed
Key collection by arrangement

Please send the refundable damage deposit of 30% of the total holiday cost, preferably a separate cheque which can be returned after the property has been checked and found undamaged.

Please send a non-refundable deposit of 50% of rental with this form and the balance to have arrived 4 weeks in advance of the first day of your holiday.

Rates per week in sterling – subject to availability

April, May, June, October, Xmas   = low season
July, September   = mid season
August   = high season

10% discounts for two consecutive weeks
20% discount for three consecutive weeks
30% discount for four consecutive weeks

Please make cheques payable to //////// and send to the address below:

USING AN AGENT

If handling the letting of your home seems too much of a headache, you may prefer to opt for the expert help of a letting agency. There are a myriad of companies offering dream villas, and many of them are actively searching for properties to add to their list. First consideration would be to find a company that operates in your locality. The initial letter of enquiry usually results in a visit from a local representative, who will soon tell you if your property is suitable for inclusion in their list. You may be shocked at the high percentage that they take and you should decide whether it is justified by their advertising and the inclusion of photos and details of your property in their very glossy brochure. If you decide you have found the right agent then you must plan well ahead. New brochures usually go to print just after the end of the summer and land on the prospective holiday maker's door-mat just after Christmas. Flicking through the pages of blue skies and luxurious villas during the bleak winter days of a British winter is usually sufficient temptation to fill the summer rental period. You may wish to compare several different companies before signing a contract. Most want an exclusive agreement for all the high season months, and if you plan to take your own holiday during that time it may take some hard negotiating. On the other hand, they are reluctant to guarantee full rental occupation even though the high season usually books quite easily. Small print on the contract will mention whether they are responsible for cancellation problems. Very few offer key-holding or cleaning services, but they may be able to recommend someone in your area who will undertake these chores for a further fee or percentage. Careful calculations will lead you to decide whether paying the agent's percentage is worth the freedom from the involvement of arranging advertising and taking bookings yourself. A full list of agents handling holiday rentals is obtainable from the Italian State Tourist Office at www.enit.it

Below is a list of some of the agents offering holiday rentals properties in Italy:

www.cottagestocastles.com
www.dolcevitavillas.com
www.homeinitaly.com
www.italianbreaks.com
www.italian-homes.com

www.italiareservations.com
www.invitationtotuscany.com
www.ownerssyndicate.com
www.qualityvillasitaly.co.uk
www.rentavilla.com
www.summerinitaly.com
www.vacanzeinitalia.com
www.villavacations.com

7

Daily Living

SPEAKING THE LANGUAGE

Learning Italian

Due to the kindness of the Italian people it is quite possible to survive in Italy without speaking their language. Needless to say it would be your cultural loss. Even minimal attempts to speak Italian will be greeted with sympathetic encouragement and approval. The use of body language is already part of the Italian's means of communication and a sense of humour is as useful as a dictionary. However, there can be no doubt that speaking Italian will enrich your daily life. Any foreigner who has chosen to spend some of their life in this delightful land must feel obliged to make efforts to adopt the equally delightful language.

Studying at home

Home study courses by printed word, audio cassettes, CD ROM or downloaded from the Internet all play their part in acquiring the first basics at a pace adapted to the individual and the time available. The BBC has a good range of courses from everyday conversational Italian through to full-length study of the language. Information can be found at www.bbcshop.com or Tel: 0191 2220381. Linguaphone, a long established name in language learning, offers everything from short courses for tourists through to a lengthy in-depth study course, which is supported increasingly with online help. Visit www.linguaphone.com or Tel: 020 83334898.

Taking a class

Intensive Italian language courses can be found in major UK cities, with the international organisations offering the opportunity to continue study in a school in Italy. The three following schools are examples.

Berlitz School of Language
www.berlitz.com
Tel: 020 7408 2474

Inlingua School of Languages
www.inlingua.com
Tel: 0121 4540204

Linguarama
www.linguarama.com
Tel: 020 74057557

Local courses

Many Italophiles attend evening classes, usually held at local colleges of education or community centres in the UK. The courses range from complete beginners to examination-orientated study. Classes usually begin in September, at the beginning of the scholastic year, and run for anything between two and seven months. After some thirty sessions of two-hour

classes most students are well on the way to conquering the
initial language barrier. Local libraries are a good source of
information for the classes available in your area.

Learning in Italy

Attending an intensive language course in Italy is the most
dynamic learning method. Most Italian cities offer language
courses for foreigners, often held in the universities and running
from April to September. Dormitory or bed-sit accommodation
is usually available or there is the ideal option of living in an
Italian family home. A full list of language schools can be found
on the online directory www.it-schools.com.

DAY-TO-DAY NECESSITIES

Shopping

Everyday life in Italy runs a very different course to that in the
UK, partly because of the opening times and partly because
shops and other facilities are simply not run in the same way.
The British queue system breaks down in the face of the Italian
shop assistant who tries to serve a little to everybody at one
time. Instead of the UK's anonymous supermarket cash desk, in
Italy the shop is a place to catch up with the latest gossip and to
exchange civilities.

In Italy shopping and daily chores are a pleasure, provided
you go about them in an Italian way. This section enables you to
do this and supplies simple information that Italians take for
granted, but that may be alien to you.

General opening hours of shops are as follows:

8.30–9 a.m. to 12.30–1 p.m., 4.30–5 p.m. to 7.30–8 p.m.

These hours apply Monday to Saturday inclusive. Sunday is
closing day for everyone except for shops selling fresh pasta and

shops selling newspapers, which open on Sunday morning. All shops have an early closing day which varies depending on the type of shop it is and also the region of Italy. Generally speaking, shops are closed on the following days (except for those in tourist resorts where they often stay open seven days a week and on public holidays too):

Monday – hairdressers, photographers, clothes boutiques and pasta shops
Tuesday or Wednesday or Thursday – food shops
Tuesday and Thursday afternoons – butchers (including those within supermarkets)
Saturday – hardware/appliances shops.

In the summer, everybody takes a three-week holiday some time between June and October, the most popular month being August. When a shop is closed for a holiday you will find *chiuso per ferie* written on the doors, usually with the date on which the shop will re-open.

Although supermarkets exist, they are often quite small and have a limited selection of produce, and shopping is mostly done in a series of individual shops. Most supermarkets are franchises of companies such as Sidis, Cral and Conad, but they are still more like grocery stores than Italian versions of Sainsbury's or Tescos. Consequently, high-street butchers, bakers and grocers are kept in business, as are other shops selling food, such as the fresh pasta shop and the *caffè* which usually produces an irresistible selection of cakes, patisserie and ice-cream as well as serving coffee and alcoholic drinks.

One of the most indispensable shops along the high street is the *tabaccherie* (tobacconist's). They sell the various necessities for dealing with bureaucracy, such as postage stamps, together with matches (which you will probably not find in either the supermarket or anywhere else), sweets, cigarettes, postcards, toiletries and a selection of gifts and souvenirs.

Something missing from the Italian high street is the

laundrette. Nearly all Italian families have washing machines at home so there is no demand except in the biggest cities and where there is a high student or tourist population, such as in Florence. Dry cleaners may offer a washing service, but you will pay well above the odds for it. If you get really desperate, search out a wash-house in a village and do it yourself.

SHOPS – useful terms

The following is a list of shops in Italian:

alimentari	food shop/grocer's
calzolaio	shoe repairer
casa di pasta	fresh pasta shop
enoteca	wine merchant's
farmacia	chemist's
ferramenta	hardware store
gelateria	icecream shop
gioielleria	jeweller's
macelleria	butcher's
mercato	market
paneficio/panetteria	baker's
parrucchiere	hairdresser
pasticceria	cake shop
pescheria	fish shop
profumeria	perfume shop
salumeria	salami and cured meats
supermercato	supermarket
tabacchi	tobacconist's
tintoria	dry cleaner's
ufficio postale	post office

Whatever you purchase while you are out shopping, whether it is a postcard or a pair of shoes, you will be given a *ricevuta fiscale* (receipt), which you should keep until reaching home in case the *guardia di finanza* (a branch of the police) should ask you to prove you purchased your goods and the shopkeeper registered the sale. This also applies to having a haircut or drinking a *cappuccino*, even though it would seem almost impossible to prove the expenditure. Should you not be given a receipt, officially both you and the seller are liable to a fine.

Banks

Italian banks are open Monday to Friday only, 8.30 a.m. to 1.30 p.m.. Some also open in the afternoon, usually between 3 and 4 p.m., although this varies slightly from bank to bank. The majority of banks operate on a local rather than a national basis, which means that services are not very wide-ranging. Note that it is very common not to write either the date or to whom the cheque is payable.

Many Italians have safes at home, usually in the wall behind a painting, and keep their money that way. Fortunately, the pressure of the EC free market has obliged banks to develop computer link-ups and install automatic cash machines which take international cards, opening up access to foreign banks. For more information on opening an Italian bank account see 'Currency and banking' in Chapter 3.

Post offices

The post office, known as the PTT or *ufficio postale*, as well as providing regular postal services, is the place where most people pay bills, transfer postal orders, collect their pensions, pay for their car tax and so on. Not surprisingly, therefore, there are invariably long queues and if you simply want to buy a postage stamp you are much better off going to a *tabacchi*.

As the post office is open government hours, generally 8 a.m. to 2 p.m. (although major post offices are open 12 hours a day), the lunch period is the quietest time to go. To send a parcel you may have to go to a special parcel post office where you must fill in a form, usually at least in triplicate, giving details of both the *mittente* (sender) and the *destinario* (recipient).

Most post offices are fussy about the way in which you package a parcel: the preferred method is to use string and a metal seal which can be purchased from a *cartolibreria* (book shop) or *tabaccherie* (tobacconist).

You may wish to use the post office to receive mail by *poste restante*. The sender should address the envelope *fermo posta* followed by the address of the post office. You will probably need to show an identity document to claim post and may have to pay a charge. The post office also send telegrams and deals with money orders.

GETTING AROUND

Italy has a fairly well-used and well-priced but poorly organised public-transport system. Strikes, delays and technical hitches regularly wreak chaos. Private transport companies are better run, but it tends to be the case that all buses and trains for the same destination leave at the same time, rendering the selection of services somewhat limited. It is hardly surprising, therefore, that most Italians travel by car.

Taking the train

The boot of Italy is almost completely girdled by railway tracks. This does little to enhance the coastline, but it makes for scenic train rides and preserves Italy's mountainous interior. The great majority of the network is owned by the *Ferrovie Statale* (State Railway), and covers nearly 20,000 kilometres with more than 3,000 stations. Trains are efficient and cheap – for example a one-way ticket from Florence to Venice is approximately £14 at the time of writing. If you are considering travelling around Italy in your search for a property, the Eurodomini ticket may fit the bill, with unlimited travel on a number of days during a month. Prices start at £118 for three days' travel, with upgrades available for first class and fast train services. If you want to travel to Italy in style, the Orient Express will take 31 hours from London to Venice and cost £1,270 one way, including meals. Information from www.orient-express.co or Tel: 0845 0772222. Normal service from Waterloo to Milan takes about 11 hours via Paris, Lille and Lyons, and return tickets cost about £180. Booking information from Rail Europe www.raileurope.co.uk or Tel: 0870 7507070.

Catching the bus

There is no national bus company in Italy, but a vast network of small companies provide an inexpensive and efficient service. Tickets are available from the bus *termini* (stations), *tabaccherie* (tobacconist's) showing the large black T sign, and at newspaper kiosks showing the sign *biglietti* (tickets). There is a confusing range of ticket types, but the main ones are a *corso semplice* (single ticket), morning or afternoon tickets otherwise described as half-day *biglietti orari* and *abbonamenti* (season tickets), which come valid for a set duration and may include tram and underground routes in cities. All tickets must be cancelled at the ticket machine on the bus.

The bright orange city buses that stoically weave in and out of the cars blocking the bus lanes are good value and worth taking if only to avoid driving and attempting to park. Rural districts are well served, although timetables are drastically reduced at the weekends. On country routes most buses will stop for you if you wave desperately at their approach and certainly you may well be grateful for a ride if your travels coincide with a train strike.

Taking the ferry

If you buy a property on the coast or on one of the northern lakes, you will undoubtedly make use of the local ferries and hydrofoils, which are an efficient and usually an enjoyable way to get around. The main sea crossings are from the mainland to Sardinia and

Sicily. There are umpteen other services to the smaller offshore islands, including the Aeolian Islands, Capri, Elba and Giglio. The northern lakes are also traversed by innumerable services, including hydrofoils, car-ferries and even steamers, as many people commute from one side of the lake to the other or travel to school that way. The list of ferry lines have informative websites and general information can be obtained from the Italian State Tourist Board www.enit.it, or, more reliably up to date, at the quayside booking offices.

Linea Lauro Tel: 081 551 3352
www.lineelauro.it

Navigazione Laghi Maggiore, Garda, Como
Tel: 02 4676101
www.navigazionelaghi.it

Navarma-Moby Lines
Tel: 0565 914133
www.mobylines.it

Maregiglio
Tel: 0564 809309
www.maregiglio.it

Flying

Italy is no longer an expensive destination for British travellers as the no-frills airlines have moved in on the scene and brought the all-frills fares tumbling down. There are also more flights from more UK airports to more Italian cities than ever before. The following list shows the main companies working from the UK to Italy.

British Airways Tel: 0845 7733377   www.ba.com
Altialia   Tel: 0870 5448259   www.alitalia.co.uk

Meridiana	Tel: 020 7839 2222	www.meridiana.it
Aer Lingus	Tel: 0818 365000	www.aerlingus.com
BMI Baby	Tel: 0870 2642229	www.bmibaby.com
EasyJet	Tel: 0870 6000000	www.easyjet.com
Volare Airlines	Tel: 01293 562266	www.volarer-airlines.com
MyTravelLite	Tel: 0870 1564564	www.mytravellite.com
Ryanair	Tel: 0871 24600000	www.ryanair.com

The Italians use internal flights far more than the British, partly due to the long distances and high mountain ranges between the most important cities. Flight time between Milan and Rome is about fifty minutes and the planes are well booked with commuting business people. Alitalia, Alisardi and ATI fly to eleven cities on the mainland and islands. Internal flights are quite expensive but there are good discounts available, such as the 50 per cent reduction for family groups.

Travelling by car

The familiar saying 'When in Rome do as the Romans do' may conjure up nightmares when taken in the context of driving in Italy. Driving around Italy requires a certain amount of courage, a sharp wit and a good deal of patience. Speed and small margins of error seem to be the essence of Italian driving. Overtaking is perhaps the worst aspect as it is often done in dangerous situations. Another nightmare of the road is the sign posting. Signs are terrible, and it can be enormously difficult to find the correct road even with a good map. Quite often the junction is signposted only at the actual turning and not in advance and there may be a collection of twenty other signs to scan through, including those of hotels, restaurants, businesses, hospitals and public services. It is far from uncommon to find two signs for the same destination pointing in opposite directions: sometimes all roads do lead to Rome!

To add to this, most roads around big towns and cities are

very busy, while the centres are positively traffic-choked. Nearly all Italians have at least one car per family, and many have two or even three. Car parking is a headache almost everywhere and when the winter brings fog and mist to the cities of northern Italy there is the problem of car exhaust-enhanced smog. When pollution levels reach an unbearable limit, cars are restricted by allowing number plates ending in an even number on the roads one day and those ending with an odd number on the next. This has unfortunately resulted in some Italians buying two cars with alternate registration numbers.

Getting around by car does, however, have its advantages, and if you intend to buy a rural property in Italy you may find that it is essential.

Fuel

Benzina (petrol) is considerably less expensive than in the UK. *Verde* or *senza piombo* (unleaded) comes in 95 and 98 octane ratings. *Gasolio* (diesel) is cheaper than petrol and is widely available. *GPL* (Liquid Petroleum Gas, LPG), is increasingly favoured, due to its lower price and environmental friendliness, and is available at petrol stations showing the *GPL* sign. However, if you are resident in Italy it may only be cheaper to run a diesel car if you travel extensively, as a higher road tax is levied.

Motorail may be the solution for taking your own car to Italy – whether on a house-hunting trip or if you are considering taking your car permanently to Italy. The cost of a return ticket to Bologna, at high peak rates for a family of four, including ferry or Eurotunnel crossings, four-bed couchette and breakfast is around £1,200. This may seem expensive until you look into the comparative costs of 2,000 miles of petrol (£175), tolls and tunnel fees (£140), hotel bills (three nights approx. £480), ferry or tunnel crossings (£300 peak price) – soon adding up to £1,100 – not to mention the wear and tear on your car and your family. For full information visit www.railsavers.com or Tel: 0870 7507070.

Taxis

The official Italian taxi is an unmistakable bright yellow, similar to a New York cab, and has a legible meter which should begin to tick away the kilometres (rather than the minutes as in the UK) as soon as you pull away. Fares are generally more expensive than in the UK, mainly because of heavy surcharges raised for extra luggage, night travel, Sundays or public holidays or any out of town destination including airports. Private cabs hang around the main railway stations, touting for work, but is best to negotiate a price for the journey before jumping in and finding an astronomical fare charged at your destination.

BUYING A CAR

In order to buy a car in Italy you must be registered as a local resident and be in possession of a *codice fiscale* (fiscal code number). An important point to check before buying a second-hand car is whether its road tax has been paid. If a car has been off the road for some time, the chances are that the road tax payments have not been maintained. If this is the case you will find that you are liable for back payments when you go to renew the road tax. Normally road tax is payable as a *bollo* (official stamp), obtainable from your local ACI (Automobile Club Italiano) office. The cost of the *bollo* depends on the power of the engine and whether it is run on petrol, diesel or gas.

Your local ACI office is the place to go for general motoring advice and also for car insurance, although it can be obtained from any insurance agent. As in household insurance, it is worth shopping around, as once you have signed you are obliged to keep with that company for ten years unless you submit six months' notice. The most common form of insurance operates on a no-claim bonus known as *bonus malus*. You may be able to get proof sent from your UK insurer to continue any no claim percentage from your last policy. Very often Italian policies are third party only and do not cover the driver but only family members in the car. Cover for the driver, *conducente anonimo*, can be taken out in the form of a supplement. Additional premiums are also required for theft and fire. Fully comprehensive insurance, *kasko*, is available, but usually far more expensive than the equivalent in the UK. Italy has one of the highest road accident rates in the EU, although the death rate is miraculously low.

HEALTH CARE

Unless you are taking up permanent residency in Italy, the usual form E111, (or E128 for students) available from UK post offices, is sufficient to cover you under the reciprocal European national health insurance scheme. It is advisable to keep it updated as European countries other than the UK have a twelve-month expiry date on their forms. To avoid any possible hitch at a time when you might not be feeling well, it is quite simple to keep it updated as long as you are paying UK National Insurance contributions. It must be renewed after any claim. The E111 covers emergency hospital treatment, but falls short of the full cost of specialist examinations, physiotherapy, X-rays and laboratory tests, dental treatment and prescribed medicines. Any bills paid should be carefully kept, as reimbursement of any payment is strictly by means of showing the officially stamped paperwork. Private insurance can be taken out to supplement treatment costs other than emergency (see list below).

www.expacareworld.net
www.ibencon.com
www.bupa-international.com

If you intend to take up residence in Italy your UK address should be registered at least one month before departure with the International Services, Inland Revenue, National Insurance Contributions, Newcastle-upon-Tyne NE98 1ZZ. Tel: 0845

9154811. Information can be found at www.inlandrevenue.gov.uk. Their leaflet, SA29 is essential reading for anyone taking up full-time residence in Italy. Once you have set the process in motion you will then be obliged to register with your local USL, *Unita Sanitaria Locale* and obtain a health number.

EDUCATION

The state system

Schooling is free from the age of three to 19 to all residents, provided they can speak Italian. Education is only compulsory from the age of six up until the age of 14, after which children generally go to a vocational school or continue with a classical education that generally leads up to university. There is a national curriculum laid down by the *Ministero della Pubblica Istruzione* (Ministry of Public Education), but management and administration are locally organised.

The school year runs from mid-September to mid-June, with short holidays at Christmas and Easter and no half-term breaks. Most classes are in the mornings, but there is school six days a week. From primary level upwards, students are expected to spend their afternoons doing homework and private study.

Low-achieving children and those with minor handicaps are integrated in normal classes, but usually have a special teacher who dedicates extra time within the class.

The following are the various schools that exist within the state system and the ages of the pupils they cater for:

- *scuola materna* or *asilo nido* – optional pre-school 3–6
- *scuola elementare* – primary school 6–11
- *scuola media* – secondary school 12–14.

To successfully complete the *scuola media* examinations, a continuous assessment of 60 per cent pass rate must be maintained throughout each year. The *diploma di licenza* media is then awarded to the successful.

At this stage there is a dividing point, with the less academic going on to *istituti tecnici* to study vocational courses leading to a diploma similar to the UK City and Guilds qualification. The academic élite stay on at school to study for the *liceo classico* or *liceo scientifico*. At 18 or 19 the successful *liceo* students take the *maturità* (equivalent to the baccalaureat). All successful students with either a *tecnici* or *maturità* are entitled to go to Italian university. The method of university teaching is similar to that in the UK universities, although exams can be postponed – almost indefinitely it seems – until the student is ready or, in the case of failure taken again.

International schools

Expatriates often opt to give their children an international school education which leads to the possibility of attending university in their home country. Lists of schools and general advice can be obtained from The European Council of International Schools, 21B Lavant Street, Petersfield, Hampshire GU32 3EL – Tel: 0730 68244 and on their website: www.ecis.org.

SUMMARY

Wherever you decide to live in Italy you can be sure that you are being given the chance to embrace life to the full. You will be playing a small role on a stage that is vastly larger than everyday life and more fun than living vicariously in a soap opera. If you should ever feel bored, it is quite sufficient amusement to sit in a café in your local piazza. You will find you are in a modern-day Roman forum where the Italians meet to talk and deal just as their noble ancestors did before them. Italy's past is part and parcel of its living present and to buy a property there is to embrace both.

Further Information

USEFUL ADDRESSES ABROAD AND UK

Italian cultural institutes

Italian Cultural Institute
39 Belgrave Square
London SW1X 8NT
UK
Tel: 020 7325 1461
www.italcultur.org.uk

Italian Cultural Institute
82 Nicholson Street
Edinburgh EH8 9EW
UK
Tel: 0131 668 2777
www.italcult.net/edimburgo

British Italian Society
21/22 Grosvenor Street
London W1X 9FE
UK
Tel: 020 7495 5536
www.british-italian.org

Italian Cultural Institute
11 Fitzwilliam Square
Dublin 2
Eire

Tel: (00353–1) 6766662
www.iol.ie/-italcult

Italian Cultural Institute
2025 M Street, NW
Suite 610
Washington DC 20036
USA
Tel: (001–202) 2239800
www.itacultusa.org

Italian Cultural Institute
686 Park Avenue
New York NY 10021
USA
Tel: (001–212) 8794242
www.italcultny.org

Italian Cultural Institute
500 North Michigan Avenue
Suite 1450
Chicago IL 60611
USA
Tel: (001–312) 8229545
www.iicch.org

Italian Cultural Institute
425 Washington Street
Suite 200
San Francisco
CA 94111

USA
Tel: (001–415) 788 7142
www.sfiic.org

Italian Cultural Institute
1023 Hilgard Avenue
Los Angeles
CA 90024
USA
Tel: (001–310) 443 3250
www.iiusa.org

Indian Cultural Institute
1200 Penfield Ave
Montreal
Quebec H3A 1A9
Canada
Tel: (001–514) 8493473
www.italcultur-qc.org

Italian Cultural Institute
496 Huron Street
Toronto
Ontario M5R 2R3
Canada
Tel: (001–416) 9622503
www.iicto-ca.org

Italian Cultural Institute
510 West Hastings St
Suite 500
Vancouver
BC V6B IL8
Canada
Tel: (001–604) 6880809
www.cvan-ca.org

Italian consulates and embassies

Italian Consulate General
          38 Eaton Place
          London SW1X 8AN
          UK
          Tel: 020 7235 9371
          www.embitaly.org.uk

Italian Embassy
          14 Three Kings Yard
          London W1K 4EH
          UK
          Tel: 020 7312 2200
          www.embitaly.org.uk

Italian Consulate
          32 Melville Street
          Edinburgh EH3 7HA
          UK
          Tel: 0131 226 3631

Italian Consulate
          111 Piccadilly
          Manchester M1 2HY
          UK
          Tel: 0161 236 9024

Italian Vice-Consulate
          7–9 Greyfriars
          Bedford MK40 1HJ
          UK
          Tel: 01234 356647

Italian Embassy
          63 Northumberland Road

Dublin 4
Eire
Tel: (00353–1) 6601744

Italian Embassy
275 Slater Street
21st Floor
Ottawa
Ontario KIP 5H9
Canada
Tel: (001–613) 2322401
www.italincanada.com

Italian Embassy
3000 Whitehaven Street NW
Washington DC 20008
USA
Tel: (001–202) 6124400
www.italyemb.org

Italian state tourism offices

Italian State Tourist Office
1 Princes Street
London W1R 8AY
UK
Tel: (071) 408 1254.
www.enit.it

Italian State Tourist Office
175 Bloor Street East
Suite 907
South Tower
Toronto
Ontario M4W 3R8
Canada
Tel: 00416 925 4482

Italian State Tourist Office
    630 Fifth Avenue
    Suite 1565
    New York
    NY10111
    USA
    Tel: 001–212 586 9249

Italian trade institutes

Italian Trade Centre (ICE)
    37 Sackville Street
    London W1X 2DQ
    UK
    Tel: 020 7734 2412

Italian Chamber of Commerce
    1 Prince's Street
    London W1B 2AY
    UK
    Tel: 020 7495 8191

Italian Chamber of Commerce
    52 Ardwick Green South
    Manchester M139 9XF
    Tel: 0161 2744168

Italian Institute for Foreign Trade
    16 St Stephen's Green
    Dublin
    Eire
    Tel: 03531 6767829

Other useful addresses

DEFRA

    1A Page Street
    London SW1 P4PQ
    UK
    Tel: 020 7904 6000

Automobile Association

    Fanum House
    PO Box 51
    Basingstoke
    Hants RG21 4EA
    UK
    Tel: 01256 469777 or
    0870 6000375
    www.theAA.com

Banca d'Italia

    39 King Street
    London EC2V 8JJ
    UK
    Tel: 020 7606 4201

Benefits Agency

    Pensions & Overseas Benefit
    Directorate
    Benton
    Newcastle upon Tyne
    NE98 1BA
    UK
    Tel: 0191 218 2000

British Council of Scotland

    The Tun, 4 Jackson's Entry
    Holyrood Road

Edinburgh EH8 8PJ
UK
Tel: 0131 524 5700
www.britishcouncil.org/scotland

Contributions Agency
Department of Social Security
Overseas Branch
Tyneview Park
Newcastle upon Tyne
NE98 1BA
UK
Tel: 0191 218 7777

Department of Trade and Industry
1 Victoria Street
London SW1H 0ET
UK
Tel: 020 7215 5000
www.dti.gov.uk

Royal Automobile club
PO Box 100
RAC House
Lansdowne Road
Croydon CR9 2JA
UK
www.rac.co.uk

Royal Scottish Automobile Club
11 Blythswood Square
Glasgow G2 4AG
UK
Tel: 0141 221 3850
www.rsac.co.uk

USEFUL ADDRESSES IN ITALY

Foreign consultates and embassies

British Embassy
Porta Pia
Via XX Settembre 80a
00187 Roma
Tel: 06 42200001

British Consulate
PO Box 679
Dorsoduro 1051
30123 Venezia
Tel: 041 5227207/5227408

British Consulate
Viale Colombo 160
09045 Cagliari
Tel: 070 828628

British Consulate
Palazzo Castelbarco
Lungarno Corsini 2
Florence 50123
Tel: 055 284133

British Consulate
Via di Francia 28
16149 Genoa
Tel: 010 416828

British Consulate
Via San Paolo 7
20121 Milano
Tel: 02 723001

British Consulate
>Via dei Mille 40
>80121 Napoli
>Tel: 081 4238911

British Consulate
>Via Dante Alighieri
>34122 Trieste
>Tel: 040 3478303

Canadian Consulate General
>Via Vittor Pisano 19
>20124 Milano
>Tel: 02 67581

Canadian Embassy
>Via G. B. de Rossi 27
>00161 Roma
>Tel: 06 445981

Irish Embassy
>Piazza di Campitelli 3
>00186 Roma
>Tel: 06 6979121

USA Embassy
>Via Vittoria Veneto 119/A
>00187 Roma
>Tel: 06 46741

British Council
>Via IV Fontane 20
>00184 Roma
>Tel: 06 478141

British Chamber of Commerce for Italy
Via Dante 12
20121 Milano
Tel: 02 876981

Ministries

Ministero della Pubblica Istruzione
(Ministry of Public Education)
Viale Trastevere 76/A
00194 Rome
Tel: 56 58491

Ministero degli Affari Esteri
(Ministry of Foreign Affairs)
Ufficio IX
Piazzale della Farnesina 1
00194 Roma
Tel: 06 36911

Youth information centres

Informagiovani
Via Alfieri Vittorio 2
15100 Alessandria
Tel: 0131 266079

Informagiovani
Via Marco Polo 53
Quartiere Navile
40131 Bologna
Tel: 051 6345550

Sportello Communale Informagiovani
Palazzo Coppa
Piazza Gransci Antonio

81100 Caserta
Tel: 0823 355561

Servizio Informagiovani
Vicolo Santa Maria
Maggiore 1
50123 Firenze
Tel: 055 218310

Informagiovani
Via Goldoni 83
57125 Livorno
Tel: 0586 899123

Informagiovanni
Via Marconi 1
20123 Milano
Tel: 02 62085215

Centro Informazioni
Documentazione Giovani
Corso Cavallotti Felice 21
28100 Novara
Tel: 0321 623270

Informagiovani
Vicole Ponte Molino 7
35137 Padova
Tel: 049 654328

Centro Informagiovani
Via Guido Da Polenta 4
48100 Ravenna
Tel: 05 4436494

Informagiovani
    Via Captain Bavastro 94
    00154 Roma
    Tel: 06 5756759

Centro Informazione Documentazione Giovani
    Via delle Orfane 20
    10122 Torino
    Tel: 011 4424977
    www.commune.torino.it

Centro Informagiovani
    Corso Portoni Borsari 17
    37121 Verona
    Tel: 045 8010795

Other useful addresses

INPS (Istituto Nazionale della Previdenza Sociale)
    Via Ciro il Grande 21
    00144 Roma
    Tel: 06 59051

Automobile Club Italiano
    Via Marsala 8
    00185 Roma
    Tel: 06 491115
    www.aci.it

USEFUL WEBSITES

www.paginegialle.it
    Italian *yellow pages* telephone directory
www.paginebianche.it
    Italian telephone directory
www.britain.it
    British Embassy in Rome

www.embitaly.it
>Italian embassy in London

www.esteri.it
>Italian Ministry of Foreign Affairs

www.noiitaliani.com
>Italian Consulate London

www.italculture.org.uk
>Italian Cultural Institute London

www.enit.it
>Italian State Tourist Board

www.payaway.co.uk/italy
>Job finder – working holidays, gap year

www.inlandrevenue.gov
>Information on living and working abroad

www.theaa.com
>Automobile Association

www.aci.it
>Automobile Club d'Italia

www.lifeinitaly.com
>Renting and buying property in Italy

www.informer.it
>General advice for living in Italy

www.noopolis.com
>Scholarship database

www.erasmus.ac.uk
>Socrates/Erasmus university exchange

www.comunetorino.it
>Youth information

www.romebuddy.com
>Travel advice for Rome

www.navigazionelaghi.it
>Crossing Italian lakes

www.hostetler.net/italy
>Italian national holidays

ABBREVIATIONS OF PROVINCES

The following is an alphabetical list of the abbreviations that are used for each of Italy's 95 provinces. You will see the abbreviations appear as the first two letters on car registration plates, in post codes and in official documents.

AG	Agrigento
AL	Alessandria
AN	Ancona
AO	Aosta
AP	Ascoli Piceno
AQ	Aquila
AR	Arezzo
AT	Asti
AV	Avellino
BA	Bari
BG	Bergamo
BL	Belluno
BN	Benevento
BO	Bologna
BR	Brindisi
BS	Brescia
BZ	Bolzano
CA	Cagliari
CB	Campobasso
CE	Caserta
CH	Chieti
CL	Altanisetta
CN	Cuneo
CO	Como
CR	Cremona
CS	Cosenza
CT	Catania
CZ	Catanzaro
EN	Enna

FE	Ferrara
FG	Foggia
FI	Firenze
FO	Forli
FR	Frosinone
GE	Genova
GO	Gorizia
GR	Grosseto
IM	Imperia
IS	Isernia
LE	Lecce
LI	Livorno
LT	Latina
LU	Lucca
MC	Macerata
ME	Messina
MI	Milano
MN	Mantova
MO	Modena
MS	Massa Carrara
MT	Matera
NA	Napoli
NO	Novara
NU	Nuoro
OR	Oristano
PA	Palermo
PC	Piacenza
PD	Padova
PE	Pescara
PG	Perugia
PI	Pisa
PN	Pordenone
PR	Parma
PS	Pesaro
PT	Pistoia
PV	Pavia

PZ	Potenza
RA	Ravenna
RC	Reggio Calabria
RE	Reggio Emilia
RG	Ragusa
RI	Rieti
RO	Rovigo
ROMA	Roma
SA	Salerno
SI	Siena
SO	Sondrio
SP	Spezia
SR	Siracusa
SS	Sassari
SV	Savona
TA	Taranto
TE	Teramo
TN	Trento
TO	Torino
TP	Trapani
TR	Terni
TS	Trieste
TV	Treviso
UD	Udine
VA	Varese
VC	Vercelli
VE	Venezia
VI	Vicenza
VR	Verona
VT	Viterbo

ALPHABET BY NAMES

The following alphabetical list is used by all Italians to spell out
words, especially over the telephone.

A	Ancona
B	Bologna
C	Como
D	Domodossola
E	Empoli
F	Firenze
G	Genoa
H	Hotel
I	Imola
K	Kursaal
L	Livorno
M	Milano
N	Napoli
O	Otranto
P	Padova
Q	Quarto
R	Roma
S	Savona
T	Torino
U	Udine
V	Venezia
W	Washington
X	Ics
Y	York or Yacht
Z	Zara

Useful Italian Words

PARTS OF A HOUSE

The following vocabulary list is made up of the various parts of a property.

angolo cottura	cooking corner
autorimessa	garage
bagno	bathroom
balcone	balcony
camera	room
camera doppio	bedroom with twin beds
camera matrimoniale	bedroom with double bed
camera singolo	bedroom with single bed
cameretta	small bedroom
camino	fireplace
cantina	cellar
corridoio	hall
cortile	courtyard
cucina	kitchen
cucina abitabile	kitchen/living-room
cucinotto	small kitchen
doccio	shower
doppi servizi	two bathrooms
doppio garage	double garage
garage	garage
giardino	garden
ingresso	entrance hall
interrato	basement

lavenderia	laundry
mansarda	attic
piscina	swimming pool
portico	porch
posto auto/macchina	parking space
ripostiglio	junk room
sala	room
salone	sitting-room
salotto	living-room
scala	staircase
soffitta	loft
soggiorno	sitting-room
soggiorno pranzo	living/dining-room
stanza	room
studio	study
terratetto	ground to roof
terrazza	terrace
tinello	small dining-room
ultimo piano	last floor
vani	room

TYPES OF HOUSING

The following vocabulary list is made up of the various terms used to describe the different types of housing.

allogio	accommodation
appartamento	flat
appartamento su due piani	flat on two floors
appartamento vacanze	holiday flat
azienda agricola	farm
bifamiliare	semi-detached
bilocale	2 rooms
3-locale	3 rooms
4-locale	4 rooms
5-locale	5 rooms

capannone	barn
casa	house
casa colonica	farmhouse
casa padronale	country house
casale	hamlet
casetta	small house
fabricato	building
fabricato rurale	rural building
fattoria	farm
indipendente	detached
monolocale	detached
palazzo	large building
rustico	rustic building
villa	detached house
villina	small detached house

PASSPORTS, VISAS AND PERMITS

certificato di equipollenza	certificate of academic equivalence
certificato di residenza	residence permit
cittadino	nationality
codice fiscale	fiscal code number
domicilio	address
firma	signature
giorno	day
nome, cognome	forename, surname
passaporto	passport
permesso di soggiorno	permit to stay
scopo lavorativo	for the purpose of work
scopo residenza	for the purpose of residence
sottoscritto	undersigned
Uffico Anagrafe	Municipal Registry Office
Ufficio Collocamento	Italian Employment Office
Uffico Imposte Dirette	Provincial Tax Office
Ufficio Stranieri	Foreign Department

valido (fino al)	valid (until)

TRAVEL

abbonamento	season ticket
Automobile Club d'Italia (ACI)	Italian Automobile Club
autostrada	motorway
benzina normale/super	regular/super grade petrol
bigliotto, biglietti, biglietteria	ticket, tickets/ticket office
Carta Verde	Youth Rail Card
conducento anonimo	unnamed driver
corso	main street, boulevard
entrata	entrance
Ferrovie Statale	State Railway System
mezza pensione	half board
Ministero del Trasporto	Ministry of Transport
numero targa	number plate
incrocio	crossroads
lavori in corso	road works ahead
passagio a livello	level crossing
pensione	boarding houses
pericolo	danger
rallentare	slow down
scheda tecnica	schedule of technical data on a vehicle
senso vietato	no entry
senso unico	one way
sosta autorizzato	parking permitted at certain times
sosta vietato	no parking
strada (privata)	road (private)
uscita	exit
verde	lead-free petrol
verde verde	higher octane lead-free petrol
viacard	motorway toll card
zona blu	parking within blue lines only

zona disco	parking within restricted times
zona rimozione	no parking: cars will be towed away
zona tutelato	no parking either side of road
vietato ingresso	no entry

MONEY MATTERS

bollo	chit or state stamp
bonus/malus	insurance policy based on no claims bonuses
buste	payslips
camera di commercio	chamber of commerce
commercialista	book-keeper, accountant
denuncia	statement; income tax return
franchigia	insurance policy with excess limit
gettone	token (eg for pay phones)
imposte	tax
ricevuta fiscale	receipt
scale mobili	wage indexation
tangenti	kick-backs, bribes
ufficio imposte dirette	provincial tax office

GENERAL

agenzia	agent, agency
alimentari	grocery stores
antiquario	antique shop
calzolaio	shoe repairer
CartaSi	an Italian credit card
cartolibreria	bookshop
casa del formaggio	cheese shop
casa di pasta	pasta shop
comune, municipio	town hall

denuncia	legal/police statement
elenchi telefonici	telephone directories
enoteca	wine merchant
fai da te	DIY
farmacia	chemist
ferramenta	hardware store
francobolli	postage stamp
gabinetti	WC
gelateria	ice cream shop
macelleria	butcher's shop
mercato	market
paneficio/panetteria	bakery
parrucchiere	hairdresser
passeggiata	evening stroll or promenade
pescheria	fishmonger
profumeria	perfumery
saldi	sales
signore, signori	ladies, gentlemen
supermercato	supermarket
tabacchi	tobacconists
tintoria	drycleaner
toiletta	WC
tribunale	magistrates court
ufficio postale	post office
vigili urbani	town police

Further Reading

GENERAL

Getting a Job Abroad, Roger Jones (How To Books, 5th edition, 2001).

Getting a Job in Europe, Mark Hempshell (How To book, 4th edition, 1999).

Retire Abroad, Roger Jones (How To books, 2002).

Fodor's Italy 2003 (Fodor 2003).

Going to Live in Italy, Amanda Hinton (How To Books, 2003).

PROPERTY

Doing Business in Italy, Dalbert Hallenstein (BBC Books, 1991).

Italian Villas and their Gardens, Edith Wharton (Da Capo Press).

REGIONAL GUIDES

Italy: Insight Guides Series (Discovery Channel, 2002).

Southern Italy, Paul Blanchard (Blue Guides, 2002).

Tuscany, Umbria and the Marches, Michael Pauls and Dana Facaros (Cadogan, 2001).

Umbria, Alta Macadam (Blue Guides, 2000).

FOOD AND WINE

Antonio Carluccio's Italian Feast, Antonio Carluccio (BBC

Consumer Publishing, 1996).

Pocket Guide to Italian Food and Wine, Spike & Charmian Hughes (Carberry Press, 1992).

Recipes from an Italian Farmhouse, Valentina Harris (Simon & Schuster, 1990).

Valentina Harris Cooks Italian, Valentina Harris (BBC Books, 1996).

Vino Italiano: The Regional Wines of Italy, Joseph Bastianich (Clarkson N. Potter, 2002).

CITY GUIDES

Florence

Florence, Alta Macadam (Blue Guides: A & C Black, 2001).

Florence: A Literary Companion, Francis King (Penguin Books, 2001).

The American Express Guide to Florence and Tuscany, Sheila Hale (Mitchell Beazley, 1989).

Rome

Venice: Blue Guide City Guide, Alta Macadam (A & C Black, 2000).

ITALIAN CULTURE

Art and Architecture

Art and Architecture in Italy 1250–1400, John White (Yale University Press, 1993).

Architecture of the Italian Renaissance, Peter Murray (Thames & Hudson, 1986).

Italian Renaissance Painting, Keith Roberts (Phaidon, 1993).

Italian Renaissance Sculpture: World of Art Series, Roberta Olson (Thames & Hudson, 1992).

Cinema

Italian Cinema, Peter Bondanella (Roundhouse Publishing, 1999).
Italian Films, Robin Buss (Batsford, 1990).

Design

Italian Interior Design Heritage, Laura Andreini (Teneues Publishing UK Ltd).

History

A Traveller's History of Italy, Valerio Lintner (Windrush, 1989).
The Florentine Renaissance, Vincent Cronin (Pimlico, 1992).
The Italian Renaissance, J. H. Plumb (Houghton Mifflin, 1990).
Italy: A Short History, Harry Hearder (Cambridge University Press, 1991).

Literature

Italian Short Stories (No. 1), R. Trevelyan (Penguin, 1965).
Italian Short Stories (No. 2), D. Vittorini (Penguin, 1972).
Italian Stories in English and Italian, Robert Hall (Dover, 1990).

Music

Italian Opera, David R. B. Kimbell (CUP, 1994).
Famous Italian Opera Arias, Ellen H. Bleiler (Dover Publications, 1996).
Italian Folk Song and Music, Luisa Del Guidice (Garland Science, 2000).

Index

We hope you've enjoyed this book and that it will help you find your dream home in Italy. You might like to know that we publish Going to Live in Italy, also written by Amanda Hinton. It deals with day-to-day living in Italy – even down to working out your electricity bills! If you think it would be useful too, you can buy it from your local bookshop or through our website: www.howtobooks.co.uk.

We try to keep our books up to date, but contact details seem to change so quickly that it can be very hard to keep up with them. If you do have any problems contacting an organisation please get in touch, and either we or the author will do what we can to help. And if you do find correct contact details that differ from those in the book, please let us know so that we can put it right when we reprint.

Finally, please give us your feedback so we can go on making books that you want to read. If there's anything you particularly liked about this book – or you have suggestions about how it could be improved in the future – please email us on info@howtobooks.co.uk.